Success in my hands

A journey to find my own
peace and freedom

Richard Cook

BALBOA.PRESS
A DIVISION OF HAY HOUSE

Balboa Press books may be ordered through booksellers or by contacting:

Balboa Press
A Division of Hay House
1663 Liberty Drive
Bloomington, IN 47403
www.balboapress.com
844-682-1282

ISBN: 978-1-4525-4791-6 (sc)
ISBN: 978-1-4525-4790-9 (e)

Print information available on the last page.

Balboa Press rev. date: 01/08/2016

Dedicated to my mum, my dad and my sister for their love and support in good times and the bad.

"I finally found what I have been looking for!"

☺ My Peace and freedom ☺

In memory of my Grandfather

Lt James Augustine Ryan 3rd Bn. Rifle Brigade

Military Cross

During the attack on St Auburt, on October 11th 1918, he showed the greatest of gallantry. He led his platoon across the open country, heavily swept by machine guns and artillery fire, and entered the enemy line. Although wounded by bomb he reorganised his platoon and held his position until relieved at dusk. His cheerfulness and disregard of danger were a magnificent example to his platoon.

Contents

Foreword

Richard has a unique story to tell. It is a story written with passion, understanding and total congruence. Like many, Richard has had to deal with the 'stuff' life throws at us. Richard's stuff was with him 24/7 and his perceived (by himself and others) disability was a constant reminder that he was different. I prefer to think of Richard as unique. This uniqueness was apparent when I first saw him as a client then was consolidated even more when he became a student. I am also pleased now that Richard has become a friend. The transformation is awesome and I encourage anyone to read his story, and to learn and understand that we are all unique in our own way and we can, like Richard, take back command over our lives and become who we dare dream to be.

'He did it because he knew he could'

Kevin Laye.

Acknowledgements

Kevin Laye
www.kevinlaye.co.uk

Thank you for giving me my life back. Stepping into 1 Harley Street in 2006 started a process of empowerment and then the beginning of a journey to see myself as I am: unique and here with a purpose. You have a blend of skills that opens the mind and enable people to change and live a better life. With just one visit, I did it because I knew I could.

Roger Callahan
www.rogercallahan.com

The founder of Thought Field Therapy. Thank you for your discovery. After 30 years of psychological challenges I can truly say these techniques were what I have been looking for! The smile from within has returned ☺

Friends

To all my friends who have known me through good times and the bad. I am grateful for their advice and support to help me face the things that I needed to change. I love them all.

To the Saints (St Helenian friends)

Thank you for the fun times, your island is special. St Helena is a gem in the South Atlantic and I am honoured to have lived there. I look forward to returning soon! ☺

Marcella Sguazzini

Thank you for editing my first book.

msguazzini@yahoo.it

My GP

Thank you for your unwavering support over the years.

Douglas Arter Centre, Salisbury.

To all the staff: you all play a significant part in my life and this has been enriched whilst working at the centre. To the members: I am proud that you are part of my life and honoured to be part of yours. To all of you: I am incredibly grateful. Also a thank you to those who bring in tins of chocolates that I have a habit of reaching into. Humbugs to those who put them in places where I cannot reach☺ You know who you are! ☺

To all the staff at Help for Heroes.

As a volunteer I am incredibly grateful for being part of such a wonderful team. Your warmth, generosity and kindness always make me feel welcome and brings a smile to my face. ☺ Thank you for making a difference!

Barbara Brunoldi

Her unique style of coaching opened a door allowed me to become whole in body and perfect just the way I am. Her extraordinary work and her passion for truth open doors that enable us to find our heart's desires and to create our own path, through unravelling life's obstacles. Because we have to be and to love ourselves just the way we are. Life is a precious present: just enjoy it. Thank you.

Photos taken by John Cassidy www.johncassidyphoto.co.uk

You are a creative genius with the camera. Through you're eyes and the lens Thank you for capturing photos, through your eyes that show I am just ME.

I hope many others feel empowered to show off their differences and feel at one with themselves, no matter who they are and what journey they are on. I also hope they will be inspired by your work and realise that your imagination and vision capture the real personality and confidence.

Finally I would like to thank my sponsors. Since all the new things start with taking the first step, this is where my journey began: to get my story published.

To Amanda Hamilton of Drink Me Chai: thank you. I am now tasting life with a new direction. A life that's now full of surprises, excitement and adventure.

www.drinkmechai.co.uk

To Sam Boyce at Timeless Ink Tattoo Studio.

Introduction

This book is about my journey since stepping out of 1 Harley Street, in April 2006. A journey to remove lifelong thinking patterns that held me back from living a fulfilling life, having been born with short arms. The book tells a story of how I have changed my way of thinking, the help I looked for to change those negative thoughts that stopped me to express myself for nearly 30 years, the tools I now use and the attitude I now have.

It is about my search for the right help and then to become a student of my own thinking and to learn how to create my life without the limits imposed on me by others, through years of social conditioning.

> *Every time you don't follow your inner guidance, you feel a loss of energy, loss of power, a sense of spiritual deadness.*
>
> **Shakti Gawain**

My journey started in 1970, after being born in Malta as my father was in the Army. The very start of it surprised everyone. My parents did not know that I was to be born with short arms so it was a shock to all. There were no scans at the time to give my parents any idea of how I was developing. Then, approximately 10 days after being born, I picked up what we understand to be a gastro virus. I would then spend 6 weeks in hospital (Bighi Naval Hospital, Malta) then flown back to the UK (Aldershot) and I was there for another two weeks.

As a child, we travelled to many different countries, with postings to Germany, St Helena and Cyprus. But, over the years, I felt a sense of difference. As a child I did not know how to express those feelings of being different but I knew that I was different to others.

The journey that I took as a child was one of wanting to hide a part of me that I felt was the difference: my arms. My arms became the centre of attention in my mind and I felt I had no control over those unpleasant feelings. We changed countries but the feelings were always the same. I felt I wanted to be away from people but yet, somehow, I mixed in well. But, in other ways, I isolated myself because of my way of thinking: those patterns of thought led to many self destructive things.

In fact, as I entered into adult life, those patterns came with me. I experienced anxiety, depression, panic attacks and I ended up drinking excessively for many years. I did not know how to change. I only knew that I wanted the thoughts to change to be able to take charge of my own life.

Now in my forties, I feel I have been given a second chance in life. The journey that I have taken shows that my thoughts disabled me, now the journey that I am on will show my thoughts are enabling me. Those thoughts come from a knowing that I was born whole in body, perfect just as I am. I then created my own path, unravelling my life's obstacles and loving myself just the way I am. ☺

> *"The most important kind of freedom is to be what you really are. You trade in your reality for a role. You give up your ability to feel, and in exchange, put on a mask"*.
>
> **Jim Morrison**

This book is about my journey to find my own peace. Being born with short arms and what I thought about them challenged me a lot in life. My father was in the Army and we moved roughly every three years. Most of my childhood was abroad. I am glad it was, I am grateful it was. I had a great time doing different things. But from an early age, I just felt different. Understandable I suppose. There was no one similar to me, so I guess I had different thoughts from other people.

I only met someone with similar arms when I was 28. Now in my 40's a new life begins. Now a second chance! This second chance has been a result of an intention to find a solution. Focusing on it to ensure it never wavered. Having the tenacity to find ways of ensuring, I would find the solution. Then when I found it, there is a sincere gratitude to those that have helped me.

I went along as many avenues as I could: but the end of each seemed like a dead end. I had to turn around and find another way to get me to where I wanted to be. Family and friends could see that I wanted my own peace. Peace with me just being me. I have no axe to grind with anyone now. More forgiving and loving of the person I am.

The journey now offers so much more than I realise. I want to lead the life that I have now as a fruitful one. Live in harmony with the flow of life, not against it.

In this journey that I have taken I was not alone. My parents didn't know that I had short arms until I was born. So, it must have been a shock. But no more of a shock, I guess, than any other parent who has a child with a physical difference. My journey from the moment I was born was going to be different. But I am glad it has been that way.

We visited many countries in my early years: a child's dream. I have a lot to be thankful for: my parents, the people I met and the army. I am proud to have found a way of changing my lifelong thinking habits. I still practice each day on keeping old thoughts at bay. I seem calmer, more self assured.

I now know that all I went through was for a reason: in the end it would give me the incentive to write this book. It gives an insight to me. Our journeys through life are all different. My journey was full of many psychological challenges along the way. But now I know it was all part of it. The journey now is different: I feel much calmer and at ease with my life's direction because I now choose it. The peace seems to have arrived. The answers I found came from within.

I was born enabled but my thoughts disabled me. I then replaced them to enable again and now this book shows how I found my peace of mind. By believing and seeing myself perfect and whole just as I am. ☺

'When you smile from within, people on your outside smile back'.

Richard Cook

Chapter I
Taking the first step

"Take the first step in faith, You don't have to see the whole staircase. Just take the first step"

Martin Luther King (1929-1968)

My first step to changing my life was by stepping into 1 Harley Street, London in April 2006. My life up until then had been one of a mental turmoil. I had unconsciously used the thoughts about my arms to hold me back.

Those thoughts had been on my mind for so long that all I wanted was a means to be set free from those unconscious thoughts. What went on behind the doors of 1 Harley Street would change my life forever. Ordinary people enter the doors, extraordinary things seem to happen there: things that help others move forward with their lives.

Maybe I looked at my life by looking at a staircase: seeing the whole but unable to see each step. The tools that helped me move forward with my life are my steps to freedom.

I just needed to take each step before moving to the next. Now I know that my life will be not only a series of steps but a series of stepping stones to a life that offers so much more. Why? Because I am taking the steps to create it!

Harley Street was to be my last option to regain control over my life. Why would I say this? Well because I had tried almost every route via the NHS. Often I would keep going back to my GP for help.

I am grateful for his help but the services provided still did not help with changing what I was thinking. All I wanted was relief from the thoughts surrounding 'my arms'.

Those were the traumatic thoughts that kept holding me back. I had seen psychologists even a psychiatrist. I had counselling yet nothing seemed to prevent the thoughts from leaving my mind!

So I eventually took it upon myself to take charge and find a solution for me. So what was so special about Harley Street? Well I feel that I went in as a person disabled by my own thinking and I left with being enabled to take charge of my life.

I felt I left with being able to start a new journey by being just me. So, where would my life go now? What would I go on doing? Who would I become? Well first of all I became a happier and my life was beginning to change for the better.

Happiness for me was a major key into moving forward. Eliminating negative thoughts was what I wanted and a set of tools was given to me to help keep the negative thoughts at bay. So what were the tools for change? Well a simple technique with an effective solution: a technique at my fingertips.

This tapping technique would become my foundation for change. Thought Field Therapy has helped me to eliminate negative thought patterns right at the root cause. No more popping pills or drinking alcohol to relieve the thoughts. No more soul destroying actions.

Thought Field Therapy has been used in Kosovo: I have included a letter in the next chapter written by the Kosovo Medical Battalion Chief of Staff to Roger Callahan, the founder of Thought Field Therapy.

I would now become fascinated by my own thinking. How could I change my thinking to become a different person? My thoughts were self destructive. I had anxiety, panic attacks and I had isolated myself from society. On and off for around 30 years.

It seemed that I could not engage in conversation with lots of different people. I always thought it was linked in with my arms. People looking at me, inquisitive not knowing, but at the same time I didn't know what was going on. I did not grow up with people similar to me. It was not until I was 28 years old that I met someone similar.

I do remember when, in 2006, I emailed Paul McKenna for help. It turned out that he did not do 'one to one' sessions anymore. I contacted him because I had seen a programme on how to change life. He has helped someone with a disability to get control of their life: I wanted to do the same.

I got a reply and it led to Kevin Laye, a good friend of his. At this point I still wasn't sure what to do. Was the chance to get help taken away? At the time I felt it had. Yet for some reason and I still do not know how this happened. An email came back from Kevin Laye. He later contacted me and I spoke about what was on my mind.

What was said over the phone made perfect sense to me. I have lost count of the many traumatic events I had had over the years. Yet each one, I guess, added and became a catalyst to preventing my life going as well as it could. A snowball effect the wrong way. Every time I tried to get a job, I got the interview but often couldn't attend: I would panic at the last minute.

I also kept going for the wrong job. Perhaps I didn't realise how much things had affected me and, going for the wrong job, was a way to stop me from moving forward.

Everything that I wanted to do was sabotaged by anxiety, panic attacks or alcohol: not a good way to go when your nerves are affected in the first place. The drink gave me a lift. But also gave me one hell of a drop. I really couldn't function.

Everything in my life was affected: my parents and even my sister bore the full brunt of what I was thinking. Somehow I just couldn't let go. My thoughts had a hold over me.

As I write this I somehow wonder why I kept going. I certainly wanted to find peace with it all. For some reason, I knew I would find a solution.

Now I realise that the very focus itself would lead to my peace: I had the right intention, found the right people, found the right tools and all this gave way to peace finally arriving ☺

I must admit I had a bumpy ride to get to where I am now. Stepping out of 1 Harley Street with a set of tools for my mind was the best investment I ever made. My life before Harley Street was like trying to be a mechanic without a set of tools to keep a car going: now I have them.

I also feel that the right fuel mixture is being added to keep me running: eating healthier foods and avoiding alcohol as much as I can is helping my performance. You might as well say that is like adding diesel to a petrol engine: at some point you are going to stop and breakdown.

Why did I take the first step into Harley Street you may ask? Well there is a saying: when you get sick and tired of being sick and tired YOU CHANGE. Change your thoughts and you literally change your life. Change your thoughts! 'Change your life' by Wayne Dyer gives an insight to this: different thinking gives different results.

Maybe it is because like thinking attracts like results. If I had anxious thoughts, depressing thoughts, for some reason I would get people, around me, who felt uncomfortable. Depressing things would happen to me: lack of work, lack of money and lack of happiness. Why would I want any of that? Surely I deserve to be free, at peace and happy. ☺

Well for some reason when letting go of my old thoughts, releasing my past, the latter seems to be happening. I have become free, more at peace and happy with being myself. ☺

So what has happened since stepping out of 1 Harley Street? Firstly I have met some great new friends. Friends that I know I can turn to for assistance. Friends that have been through troubled times and yet moved forward to a new life. Allowing more, pushing less.

I was always pushing and being pushed back: one step forward, two steps back. Now it seems there is one step forward, then another step forward and so on. Always moving forward and just being happy with the process.

Guided by intuition I guess, I do what feels right and I leave what feels wrong and I correct myself in order to follow the right thing. It's much like a plane. it is always being corrected along its flight path. I guess I am no different: I am setting the destination, but with the tools I now have, I can decide how quickly I want to get there.

The day I stepped out of Harley Street and went to see my parents my mother knew I had done the right thing. She saw that I had come back as a different person. I do remember her saying once that she had 'finally got her Richard back.'

I guess she recognised the person I use to be before I had the anxiety, depression and panic attacks: someone full of life and enjoying being himself. By trying to fit in with other people, I was no longer myself. I am me. Still physically different, yes. I cannot change that. But I can change how I view it to lead the life I want: that's all had to do ☺

So, what happened in Harley Street to enable me to move forward the way I have? I kind of knew about the tools I had been given. I had done Reiki, I acknowledged acupuncture and meridians, but I never thought that the tools I was to be given could literally change my life.

This book would not be written if I didn't have them. A volume called 'Tapping the healer within' by Roger Callahan, sat on my book shelf for nearly 5 years before going into Harley street. I never really read it from cover to cover. Within it, there are a set of tools that I use each day: I just did not know how to use them. Or, simply, I wasn't ready to use them.

Kevin Laye did and I was to go on using them and still do to this day. TFT or Thought Field Therapy is incredible: I use it everyday and I am so grateful. These tools have kept me going and moving forward to a peaceful me☺

I still haven't found out what gave me the courage to keep going. Something within me knew I would get there in the end. By doing it my way, I guess, even with a lot of setbacks along the way.

To me, each set-back is only temporary. And if something is temporary, it can therefore be changed. So setbacks to me were always a short term thing. Of course, I have had my occasional hold-ups since Harley Street. I know they were my own doing, slipping back into an old pattern of thinking by not using the tools. My responsibility to use them!

I was given them for a very good reason: to keep me alive. Had I kept going in my old way of thinking, the inevitable would have happened. The alcohol and poor health would have taken me in the end.

Harley Street has given me the means to step on to a life of learning. I seem to be interested in my own thinking. I seem more aligned to achieving my goals. This is the reason why I feel I am succeeding. Doing something at last that feels right to me. Changing my thinking and giving myself a sense of purpose.

When I had low energy thoughts, the anxiety and depression would appear. If the anxiety and depression were the result of unhappy thoughts, then all I had to do to feel better was to have happier thoughts. But in order to do so, I would need to shift my thinking and find something to feel happier and content about.

Strangely enough, after years of people commenting on my arms in a negative way, I would now think differently about them. I would get to love them. I started acknowledging them as a part of me that I liked. Now I do. ☺

I can laugh about having short arms. I know it may look awkward but making a joke about such things makes them look easier. Laughing seems to change my perception straight away. It's like flicking a switch that changes mood and releases a better feeling.

By taking the first step, I took control. No more having others give me advice and I just follow it out of a sense of urgency. It is my life but what I wanted for me was a direction and a reason for taking that direction to the success. I give myself a bit more time to think now, more time to make decisions and I give myself time to act in the right way.

This book started by taking a step into Harley Street, a journey that was positive and enlightening for me. I somehow knew I would find a sense of peace. But not quite in the way that it is turning out to be.

What I realised is that, as a very small child, I was without the anxiety, depression and panic attacks. So how did they arrive? Also if they were not there in the very beginning of my life, maybe I could get myself back to that very same state of mind but with the tools I have now.

Obviously the anxiety, depression and panic attacks came through different traumatic events: people touching my hands, looking or bullying at school created much of it. I was not confident enough to deal with the physical difference then. I could only give answers like: 'I was born like that'. The sense of difference was always there. Now I am proud of that difference.

TFT removed these negative feelings and then I found ways of creating feelings of peace with the difference. ☺ Getting back to where I was when I was a small child when I just did things. When I didn't really know any difference, I just lived it. Being me.

Has stepping out of Harley Street given me the chance to live my life by just being me? I certainly think so. By trying to fit in with what other people expected, I was bound to get anxious and depressed. I simply just could not be me. I was trying to be like everyone else. I was taking on other people's thoughts and not giving myself the time to create my own.

Months and years have gone by since stepping out of Harley Street but I no longer feel afraid. I can do, with ease, simple things like going into a coffee shop. I always used to go in so tense, felt awkward and, in one respect, I felt that I was alone with my thoughts.

I disliked handing money over because of my hands, but now I enjoy just being me. Changing my thoughts has simply given me the sense of freedom to be myself. That is what I wanted and it appears to be what I am having. Later on in life, I know.

What I have noticed is that the happier I am, the more likely I am to attract happier circumstances into my life. Life is like a mirror: whereas I was unconsciously attracting the bad stuff, now—with the help of the tools I have been given—I am attracting the good stuff instead. The 'good stuff' means that my health returns as I drink less. It means that I take greater care of this one body that I have. Getting fit and going to the gym more. At the height of my mental turmoil there were times when I couldn't even go outside of my own home.

Stepping out of Harley Street certainly started the process of disabling my old thoughts. I now create enabling ones. The enabling thoughts lead me to a more energetic self. Now I realise how much of my life went by without it.

Stepping into Harley Street was like taking cover from a life of mental turmoil. Taking cover gave me a choice and the time to choose: step out and not use the tools given from within and almost certainly die or step out and use the tools from within and start living.

The choice was mine. No one else could do it for me. They are not me: I am me, it is my life. I wanted the best for me and I did it. I got the best. Not just the best, but a life saving set of tools.

Now I'm in my forties and I can say that I've spent most of my life not performing to the best of my ability. Negative thinking and almost certainly alcohol was the key factor in it all. How that has changed and, along with this, something big had to happen.

> *When you affirm big, believe big and pray big, putting faith into action, big things happen."*
> **Dr. Norman Vincent Peale 1898-1993,**
> **Preacher and Author**

For many years I felt that I knew I would find my own path to peace. It was going to be a big challenge yet I knew it was possible. I was always focusing on wanting to change. I never gave up hope. I never quit looking for the right tools to live my life the way I wanted.

The peace NOW is the biggest thing that has ever happened to me. ☺ It is something that takes some time getting used to. I have questioned it many times, wondering why I deserve to have it. But I have kept going. Maybe in essence I do deserve it. It is rightfully mine. It was rightfully mine many years ago: I just got distracted from it through a series of events and not knowing how to cope.

There are other things I have done since taking my first step. Public speaking, telling my story to others in front of over 100 people :I guess it was on my list, at some point. I felt that I wanted to help in some way. I even used my tools given to me at Harley Street: what a difference that made! I was telling my story with a smile as now I 'm free from it all. ☺

The idea of writing a book was mentioned in the room of 1 Harley Street. There is a saying that 'Thoughts Become Things'. Well I thought about writing a book for a few years, not necessarily in the time since Harley Street. More like 10 years ago. Whether I was ready then I have no idea, probably not.

I hadn't developed my skills in my own thinking at that time. If I had started writing in the depths of my own despair, I am sure it would not have been published. I had to be in a different place mentally to enable it to happen.

I am much more detached from my traumas, now. I certainly am in a much happier place. I am calmer and more self assured. I believe in myself, believing that the idea that I have in mind will become a reality. The book, by the time it is published, will be a reality. I am astounded by what has happened since taking my first step.

Job hunting and keeping a job was always difficult before Harley Street. I even spent years in education to ensure that I would have the same opportunities as others. Perhaps I did. I just not have the rights tools to socially succeed: I somehow was out of touch with reality.

I wanted things so much that I perhaps pushed them away: anxiety can do that in most cases. Having anxiety made other people anxious around me. Only those who knew me well realised that I was trying to deal with something that I had no control over, something that was in my mind.

Moreover, the jobs I went for were not really something I had a passion for. Disability was something I knew in the end I would go back to. I just needed to be clear in my mind and be free from my own traumas.

About a year after leaving Harley Street I got a job as a Support Worker, assisting people with Cerebral Palsy at the Douglas Arter Centre, Salisbury. I at first did not know how to deal with this new type of disability yet caring for others, was to be a way forward in my life. To detach from my own selfishness as it were and start giving back what I knew.

But in some way just did not know how. Now I know how. The tools I have been given allow me to do so. I am giving my time to help other people with disabilities move forward with their lives. I am much happier in my life and, in some cases , I can see that happiness rubs off. The smile on other people's faces reveals all. ☺

I feel free at last. The feeling seems to be one that is staying. One that I hope stays with me for the rest of my life. People have fought wars for freedom and still are.

I have had so many battles over the years with my thinking. Those battles may have been worth fighting in one way, yet if the tools were provided at an early age, there is a question that I have in mind. Would I have had to fight? Well the answer to that is a straight no. I have the opportunity now to live a great life.

I feel now I can choose what to do with my life. I have become fascinated with my own self development. It is something that I enjoy so much. I seem to be smiling everywhere I go. ☺

I have found a deep sense of relaxation. Self hypnosis certainly helps me, it helps those that I interact with. And it works! My difference seems to be of no significance to me. Yes, some things that I do may look awkward.

But I now take my time to slow things down without anxiety. In some cases I just laugh at things. There are plenty of 'short arm one liners' that I come up with.

Something I have found interesting is giving directions to people. My right hand points left and my left, right. Now, try to work out how to give directions! I have seen people take the wrong turning pretty much straight away. ☺

For some reason I can see the funny side of things now. A few years ago if people mentioned my hands I couldn't deal with it: I literally clammed up and went within myself. Not a good place to be. It was very dark. A darkness that I hope will never return.

Still it has taught me something: to be compassionate with people. Their faces often tell a story if I take the time to connect with them. Mine as well told a story when people wanted to connect with me.

I just did not connect in the right way. I was afraid. Now I trust. Trust that everything will be ok. This is something that I guess I had to learn. I just had to think different thoughts, less traumatic ones and more peaceful ones. ☺

Something that strikes a note now is that how distant I was from being present with myself. I was in effect misaligned with my thinking. So out of touch with reality at times that no wonder I was not getting there: I was on automatic pilot for destruction.

I felt I wanted help but no one could. I tried pretty much every avenue, the last being Harley Street. Looking back, I have realised I have been through one hell of a ride. I was like a hurricane.

I would sometimes feel the calmness of it through alcohol and staying away from certain situations. Then, as that calmness disappeared, I was in the thick of it. No one liked being near me then.

I suppose stepping out of 1 Harley Street was like stepping into a new era in time. Being me. I felt that the old had now been replaced with someone new. I could start living. I learned to judge and feel resentment growing up through others. Now I can change it all just be in peace and awe of the world I live in.

I am grateful that I now have that chance. I see things with a clearer state of mind, experiencing them with lucidity rather than in a perpetual state of fogginess.

Being present is part of me being at peace. This is something that I guess when walking out of Harley Street I would find for myself. But I would have to do this by using the tools that were given to me. As I grew up I took on board others thoughts of me: I had no real control of my life from a conscious perspective. I was always on an unconscious automatic pilot.

I took many different steps to get the right help for me. When I look back, the step to Harley Street was probably one that was always there. I just had to find it. It was much like finding a needle in a haystack, but when you do find it, you wonder how you did it. I certainly did it when trying to find my peace.

Taking the first step was not just a step to resolving one thing. Each step from then on enabled me to unravel what was in my mind. Each traumatic event I could keep reliving, if I decided to.

But having learnt to use TFT I can hone in on the event and reduce its impact on my life. I use the tools to help me keep in control: it takes a daily practice. I guess these tools are much like what a mechanic would use when learning. First I had to remember which tool to use. Then I would remember each day to pick up the right tool for what was on my mind. Then, after a while it became automatic.

Harley Street was to be my last option to regaining control over my life. Why? Because I had tried almost every route via the NHS. Over the years I had been on anti depressants: I was walking around in a zombie like state. Experiencing heavy sweating and palpitations! Would medication give me the means to change? No, I still did not have the skills to control my thinking. And that was what I was looking for!

I have had counselling, both privately and via the NHS, but there seemed to be no real progress.I seemed to be falling into wells all the time. I would often come away with a relief that the talking was over but the unconscious part of my mind was repeating the same old pattern.

The two parts of my mind were not working together to get results. I was unconsciously going about the things in the wrong way. I had to work things out from an inside out approach.

Change the way I think and the things I think about change. Now I realise my thinking was so much like a computer:a series of mind viruses had been added to my mind and now I had to find a way of deleting each virus. It is worth reading 'Virus of the Mind' by Richard Brodie to gain an insight to this.

Growing up, I had people commenting on my arms and I conditioned myself to think about myself through the eyes of others. I now had to tap into a new set of skills to ensure the conditioning that I had been so accustomed to could be undone. Why would I want to live my life the way other people expect me to live?

I had taken on board a set of thoughts that would make my life a series of challenges to overcome. Disability would now become my own unique ability. I decide who I want to be. I take command over my life. Stepping out from Harley Street set me up to re-define myself.

Become a freeman with a saying 'A freeman on the land, looks to the horizon and sees the sunset and is grateful for all that has come his way that day.'

I felt that Harley Street had given me the first step to a new life: I now had to decide what steps to take and define them for myself.

For me the key to what I wanted was my happiness. I had it as a very young child. The essence of who I am was there when I was born. I had to find a way of getting it back. Perhaps being born with short arms gave me an inner strength that has taken me 40 years to recognise. The human spirit is there: I just never acknowledged it until now. But I am glad it has taken years to realise. It now means that I feel I can set my mind to accomplish anything I choose to do. It seems as if there is an inner compass that is always set to my true North.

That true North being the authentic me. I need no other person to tell me how I should live my life. I had taken on board over the years a sense of sadness at the fact that other people wanted to diminish my true self.

I had to change that to ensure that I now had control over my life. No more disabling thoughts, more enabling and empowering thoughts to do good whenever I can.

If sadness was something that I had become accustomed to because of old social conditioning then the opposite that I would become accustomed to would be happiness. I just needed a set of tools to flick the switch. Then operate with a thinking pattern that kept me thinking happy thoughts.

Thought Field Therapy seemed to be the answer, enabling me to flick the switch. By tapping known meridian points whilst thinking and feeling the emotion, I seemed to be eliminating the issue. At its root cause!. It seems to work. In fact I know it worked. ☺

I use it each day and I have benefitted so much from it. No more anti—depressants, no anxiety in specific areas of my life and my health seems to have improved. My medical records show it anyway. I seem to much more in control of my life.

A new direction can be set for the rest of my life. A direction with an intention to help others! Something I had always wanted to do. But how could I have helped others in the past when I needed help myself in first place? It seems that now I have found a sense of peace of mind with the physical body. I have happiness and contentment is all around me.

Actually it was always there: I just got disconnected from it. Now I appreciate the fact I am different and unique. The difference and uniqueness will now shape a new life for me. The tools that I now have help me take each step, one at a time, as I move forward with my life.

A few years ago I emailed Paul Mckenna. I was asking for his help, having seen 'I can change your life.' It turned out that he no longer did 'one to one' consultations. But below is the copy of the email. This email somehow was forwarded to Kevin Laye who later contacted me. I then went on to take the first step at Harley Street.

Dear Paul

RE: NLP and TFT

I have seen your programmes on 'I can change your life' and read your books, 'Instant confidence' and 'Change

15

your life in seven days'. I have also recently seen your programme when you helped a person with Tourettes reduce his anxiety and increase his confidence and self esteem through your techniques, which I am extremely interested in and I would like your help to change my life.

Firstly I shall give you a brief overview of myself to give you an idea of my background and experiences.

I am 36 years old and have what could be deemed in some people's mind as a disability. I have short arms similar to the old thalidomide type impairment. The medical term is congenital dysmelia. Who came up with that term I have no idea!

I didn't meet anyone with a similar impairment until I was 28, purely as there are so few and because much of my childhood was abroad due to my father being in the army. I have lived abroad and met many different people from all walks of life and subsequently developed a way of coping over the years in various situations.

My way of dealing with this mainly was to avoid them in the first place. So subsequently became anxious in a number of social situations.

This self consciousness has led to what I would describe as a fight/flight response. Looking back I think I know where some of my anxiety has started from. In 1978, I lived on a small island called St. Helena in the South Atlantic Ocean and I remember my first day at school. I was introduced to the class and all the kids looked at me and I immediately associated this with my arms and I ran out and joined the class only a few days later.

There are many circumstances over the years where this behaviour has continually been repeated which I find difficult to control as the thoughts are too quick giving me little time to relax and approach things differently to achieve a new outcome.

In certain situations I feel uncomfortable and prevent myself from confronting them as I seem to have a projected self image of my arms in front of me which I feel uncomfortable about. This creates the anxiety in the first place thus preventing me from achieving certain things in life.

Part of me has coped by denial of the difference and have over compensated by proving to everyone that I could achieve as much as anyone else. Such events have been the London marathon, Three Peaks challenge, Paralympic swimming trials in 2000.

I enjoy life and have travelled over the years. However, even when travelling, the same thinking patterns are repeated. Subconscious thoughts seem to hinder me and limit the enjoyment of being in a new place and meeting new people.

Looking back to when I was at secondary school, I joined a school band and the practices and live performances where occasionally filmed on video. On one occasion, I saw myself for the first time on the video and it created an uncomfortable feeling about myself. Although I carried on in the band I always felt self conscious.

I have had counseling in the past, both through the NHS and privately and do not mind passing on any notes from my GP if necessary. I am at the moment taking medication (sertraline) which limits the anxiety, however at some stage wish to stop taking them as I know being able to change my thinking in the first place can stop the anxiety.

I have done a bit of meditation and REIKI and read numerous self help books, I also understand the psychology of disability as I have worked for two companies who specialise in disability. However, I have yet to master my own thoughts and restrict myself by having some internalised negative thinking.

I have very few regrets in life as much of what I have done over the years has been a journey of self discovery. However I have realised that by understanding my thinking and changing the way I think, I will be much more comfortable as a whole person instead of always reflecting on a part of me physically I cannot change nor do I wish to.

I am allowing the difference and the thought processes that I have learned over the years to control me. Now I am looking to gain a more purposeful control over my life and move forward in leaps and bounds, after nearly thirty years of similar thinking patterns. I would be grateful and over the moon if you could help change the way I think.

Regards
Richard Cook

In such a short space of time over last four years, I have managed to redefine myself. From a person who once, on a few occasions, could not step out of the door to a person who now opens doors to wherever I want to go. I even find that inspiring! Astounded by my own progress, I appreciate all that comes my way.

Each step that I take offers so much more than the last. I have found a way to look forward but being present along the way. Each step I acknowledge those who help me and those that believe in me. The self belief now forms my new direction.

Something intrigued me from my conversation with Kevin Laye. After all these years I had finally realised that someone understood my own thinking.

Whilst he did not know me personally and would not have known how I lived my life for so many years, he knew how to help me to become the person I wanted to be. The way he described how I was thinking was that if I thought of my mind as a computer. Then I had a virus in it. That virus would keep running over and over again until I did something about it.

That virus was this thought relating to my arms. It had pretty much got into every area of my life. But I now had a tool to delete the virus as it were and learn how to replace it with better programmes that were more in keeping with the person I am. A kind and compassionate human being, someone who wants to do good with all that he has learnt.

Someone who wants to live his life on purpose, give back to those who need it. What a relief though it was to hear that someone finally understood me after nearly thirty years of emotional turmoil.

Why did I keep going? Well I guess I knew I would find the answer in the end. Although it has taken years, I just knew I could do it. Looking back there must be one hell of a trail of information that I have obtained. All catalogued in my mind. There was this focus to find an answer almost at any cost. My life came first, no matter what.

Even when I felt that I had lost hope there was a little glimmer of light. That light filled the darkness, an area at a time. Now this no longer exists. I just see things differently. Find new ways to get through things when previously I would find a hole and dig deeper. As I dug deeper, the darkness followed. So NOW I ensure that I feel enlightened by being myself and seeing things through my own eyes.

It is like I have discovered something that no one else has. The resilience was always there. It was just part of me and perhaps still is. Maybe it is something natural to me. By being resilient, I feel I can empower myself. The empowerment process makes me feel good. Feeling good seems to be the essence of moving forward. Good things seem to happen. Things seem to get better and better.

Not long after leaving Harley Street I wrote this testimonial.

Prior to the use of NLP/TFT and hypnosis

I am 36 years old and have what could be deemed in some people's mind a disability, I have short arms similar to the old thalidomide type impairment.

I didn't meet anyone with a similar impairment until I was 28, purely as there are so few and because much of my childhood was abroad due to my father being in the army.

Over the years I subsequently developed a way of coping in various situations. My way of dealing with this mainly was to avoid them, in first place as I felt self conscious and didn't want people asking questions. So I subsequently became anxious in so many social situations.

This self consciousness has led to what I would describe as a fight/flight response. There are many circumstances over the years where this behaviour has been continually repeated and it was almost impossible to control, due to the anxiety and stress.

Subconscious thoughts seemed to hinder me and limit the enjoyment of being in new places and meeting new people. I have had counselling, been on medication and I am sure my GP has been as frustrated as I have in not getting the problems resolved. My journey to find an answer to change the way I think and deal with various social interactions has been a long one and I am glad and proud to say the answer is using Thought Field Therapy/ NLP and hypnosis.

Since using Thought Field Therapy

Since using thought field therapy there have been instant changes in my life, I feel happier and calmer. I feel in control and confident that the changes are for the best. The old thoughts about the way I look have gone. I am no longer self conscious, I am more self assured.

The negative feelings associated with certain situations have gone and my outlook to life is always positive. I also find new ways of making things happen to achieve a positive outcome. This one treatment with Kevin has given me the tools to enable me to function at a new level, with confidence and with a relaxed state of mind . . . I hope many more people from all walks of life get the chance to use this wonderful technique and live life to the full . . . Many thanks!!

Regards
Richard

As I feel happier, my sense of humour around my own physical difference is beginning to show more and more. I find it easier to even joke about having short arms and play on it a bit and why not! Even in the local supermarket good things happen. Added this on facebook:

"Just used the self service checkout at Sainsburys! Like it! Staff helped with the packing and even with putting the money in the coin slot! How cool is that? Yet another advantage of having short arms! ☺"

Forgot to add she even put the change back in my wallet. ☺

So looking back to taking the step into Harley Street what were my steps to getting there. I could have easily changed my mind and I knew this would be the right step to take.

My Stepping Stones for change:

Having the Intention to change my thoughts

Setting an intention to do something for myself gave me more determination. That intention may have been set in my teenage years but consciously acknowledged it in the last few years. The intention itself felt right for me. Rather than saying it was a goal of mine, an intention has more energy. I began feeling that I would get there in the end. With an intention I began believing in myself. As my thoughts began to change, I could clearly see that others were acting in a more loving way towards me.

Directing my thoughts

So which thoughts do I think are more productive? The thoughts that hold me back or the thoughts that propel me forward? I for once am enjoying the new happier me. I create thoughts that now enable me to make a difference and help others.

So how do you think I have managed to do this? Well, having experienced the non-productive side of my life, I am learning to change to experience the productive side. The tools for change were there: I just had to find them.

Also I had to find someone who could help me with those tools. I did it in the end. If negative thoughts produced negative results, I finally learned how to direct positive thoughts to give positive results. My thoughts now changed direction ☺

Being Tenacious

Having found the tools to help me, I needed to use them! Each time something came up from my past, I had to find the right technique to use. I would sometimes even email back to Kevin for some more advice. It was more of a case of eliminating the emotions of the pasts as they bubbled up in my mind. Then I could create new thoughts that would help me move forward. The tools have effectively taken me from disabling to enabling in a relatively short space of time.

I would also read more on Thought Field Therapy to find out possible causes of my emotions and what I was doing to prevent myself from moving forward. The use of alcohol certainly masked my anxiety and made things worse. But once I understood what I was doing things changed.

Gratitude

Something that I always feel is gratitude to those that helped me. I am thankful for others taking their time to open a door for me. Harley Street was a door that I went into feeling disabled by my thoughts, Harley Street was a door on leaving I felt enabled by my thoughts.

Changing my thoughts has changed my life! ☺ ☺

Chapter 2
Tools for my mind!

'We cannot solve our problems with the same thinking we used when we created them'

Albert Einstein (1879-1955)

I now have a toolbox kept for my mind! To me a wonderful set of tools and techniques that enable me to flow through life: they range from simple techniques at my fingertips to viewing things in a different way. I had to find different ways of thinking about 'my arms'. New thoughts that would enable me to detach and feel content with being at ease. The tools for my mind do just that: enable me to feel at ease and at peace. ☺

The tools given to me at Harley Street and from the courses I have subsequently been on, have helped me to break free from my past. I had always wanted to resolve my thinking of the past and, I guess, that desire has been realised and fulfilled.

> *'The first principle of desire—knowing what you want.*
> *Desire is the planting of the seed'*
> **Robert Collier.**

For many years I knew I wanted my own peace with my difference. I knew I would find it in the end. I did everything I could think of and I found it. My way! Over the years, I had sown many seeds to get to where I am now. Perhaps some were seeds of self sabotage, especially during my childhood. People commenting in a negative way led me to think negatively at a deeper level. I then kept sowing more destructive seeds, to such an extent I was probably doing this in my sleep!

I planted many other seeds to ensure I would survive in a world where I felt I was the only one with short arms: that world would last for twenty eight years until I saw what I would call a double of me. With the desire to feel at peace, I guess I would want to find others similar to help me with it. Eventually I did meet someone similar: it helped but only to realise that I was not the only one. I had yet to get the answer to change my thought patterns. So, the seeds planted in my childhood that would sabotage much of my life, were ones of fear and anxiety. To change this I had to plant new seeds. 'Hybrids' I would call them. The hybrids would then help me to create a better life for myself. Be in harmony with life instead of fighting against it. I had done enough of that for over 30 years: I was tired of it!

So how would I start to live my life in harmony with it? I made a choice! The choice was to start a new way of thinking with the tools I had been given. I would also go on to learn how to use more tools for my self—development and still do. I am fascinated by the results: to me they seem miraculous.

> **If you focus on results, you will never change. If you focus on change, you will get results.**
>
> **Jack Dixon**

So what have I focused on to change? Which techniques do I use?

The very first technique that has had a profound impact in my life is the use of a meridian therapy called Thought Field Therapy or TFT, discovered by Roger Callahan www.RogerCallahan.com.

Thought Field Therapy

This has, in a short space of time, given me a means of eliminating the emotions of my past. The memory is there but the negative emotions have gone. Anxiety, depression and panic attacks literally have been eliminated. Those that have known me over the years can see the difference. For me, my whole life has changed.

It gave me the vehicle for moving forward, a chance to live in peace and start creating new thoughts to a better life. I had now found a way out, away from medical drugs and a lifeline that I could now use for myself. Pulling a peaceful and free me into my life now. ☺

For nearly thirty years I had experienced anxiety, depression and panic attacks. Now with these tools I have eliminated them: for me these experiences are over. People said I 'suffered' from these. Well now I say I have 'experienced' them as bad as they were. My reason by changing the language is that I take charge of it. I no longer feel a victim.

If I call them experiences, I can look at them from a different perspective. I now feel empowered to do something about them and move forward.

And to do so, I had to learn how to empower myself. Learn about moving from a victim state of mind to one of empowerment and beyond.

What would I be able to do by feeling empowered? Feeling empowered has given me a sense of control over my life. That's a great feeling! ☺ I make my own thoughts now, whereas, for years, I had absorbed others. This book is being written because I feel empowered.

Those old thoughts of me have gone. A more care-free person arrives and can do it just because he believes he can. That self-belief has come about through getting rid of old emotions that now do not serve me. TFT has enabled me to put a brake on my thought patterns, take cover and give me space to create a new life.

The TFT took a bit of getting used to, at the start. TFT is like removing each layer of the onion until you get to the heart of the matter. In this way, the individual traumas associated with my physical condition were being eliminated.

The panic attacks disappeared. The anxiety disappeared. The drinking became less. I felt so different, pardon the pun! ☺ Yet my world was changing in an instant: it was like the real me was being revealed. I am so proud to have given myself the chance to use these techniques. They have literally saved my life.

I have read a few books on TFT. 'Tapping the Healer within' by Roger Callaghan was the first. I have included others at the end of the book. Toxins are also talked about in his books: I now realise that toxins play a major impact on my emotions. Alcohol was one of them and certainly had been a problem in my life for many years. Actually, it was literally destroying my nerves. How could I start living a better life if I was filling a petrol driven car with diesel?

The alcohol was being used to mask my anxiety. But with TFT I began eliminating the need to have it. The real me was being uncovered by peeling away the onion. And yes, tears did roll, if that's what you are thinking. ☺

Now in my forties, I look back at when I gave the testimonial: I see significant changes. To me it seems like a miracle. Undoing years of poor thinking based on the experiences that I had as a child, makes me feel that

I have changed as a human being. TFT is now a part of my life. It helps me and I know it help others. ☺

So how can I explain what TFT is? Well, if I thought of my mind as being a computer then all the 'stuff' that has had such a negative impact on me could be called a 'virus'. My mind was literally being bombarded with viruses that stopped me from functioning as a happy human being.

Well TFT seems to remove the virus and to enable me to function again: it's like having your own virus software. 'Virus of the Mind' by Richard Brodie gives a better insight to how I may have been affected by external influences and other people's thoughts about me.

What would I need to do to remove the virus? Well the technique goes like this.

I would need to think about the issue that was on my mind. For example if I was anxious of going into a coffee shop I would think about it. Rate the feeling on a scale of 1-10 (10 being the worst) then tap the following points to reduce the feeling and enable me to feel less anxious so that I could go in.

For anxiety, I would tap using two fingertips these parts of my body whilst still feeling the emotion. (See Callahan diagram for reference to where to tap)

Anxiety

These parts of the body are tapped, in the following order, approximately six times.

- Under the eye
- Under the arm on the side of the body 4 inches down
- Collarbone point (inner end under the knuckle)

Then I would tap the back of the hand by the little finger knuckle continuously (see Callahan diagram for tapping what is called the gamut spot) and do the following.

Close eyes

Open Eyes

Look down to the left

Look down to the right

Roll the eyes one way then the other Hum a few bars of happy birthday Count 1 to 5 aloud

Hum a few bars again

Then tap again the following points.

- Under the eye
- Under the arm on the side of the body 4 inches down
- Collarbone point (inner end under the knuckle)

If during the process the feelings did not change, having tapped the above sequence, I would then tap the side of my hand (karate chop point) PR spot for what is called psychological reversal (negative polarity). I would tap this approximately 10 times then go through the process all over again.

There are other tapping points for different negative experiences. The 'trauma algorithm'—as it is called—is one that I use more often. The traumas of my past experiences now being eliminated so that I could move forward.

For the Trauma related experiences, I would tap using two fingertips, these parts of my body whilst still feeling the emotion. (See Callahan diagram for reference to where to tap)

Trauma

These parts of the body are tapped in the following order approximately six times.

- Above the eye on the inner end of the eyebrow
- Under the eye
- Under the arm
- Collarbone
- End of index finger (on outside edge by the nail)
- Collarbone
- End of little finger (on outside edge by the nail)
- Collarbone

Then I would tap the back of the hand by the little finger knuckle continuously (see Callahan diagram for tapping what is called the gamut spot)

Close eyes

Open Eyes

Look down to the left

Look down to the right

Roll the eyes one way then the other Hum a few bars of happy birthday Count 1 to 5 aloud

Hum a few bars again

Then tap the following points again.

- Above the eye on the inner end of the eyebrow
- Under the eye
- Under the arm
- Collarbone
- End of index finger (on outside edge by the nail)
- Collarbone
- End of little finger (on outside edge by the nail)
- Collarbone

Tap the back of the hand by the little finger knuckle continuously

Using eyes only look at the floor and roll the eyes directly up to the ceiling

If during the process the feelings did not change having tapped the above sequence, I would then tap the side of my hand (karate chop point) PR spot for what is called psychological reversal. I would tap this approximately 10 times then go through the process all over again.

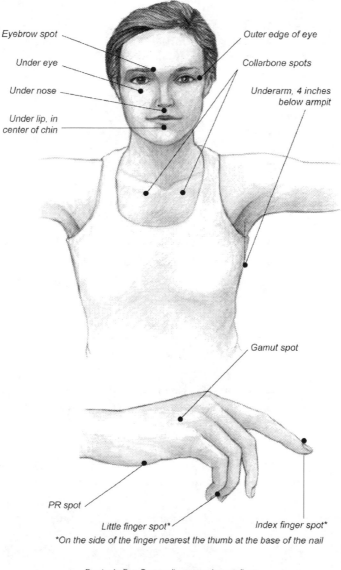

Eyebrow spot

Under eye

Under nose

Under lip, in
center of chin

Outer edge of eye

Collarbone spots

Underarm, 4 inches
below armpit

Gamut spot

PR spot

Little finger spot*

Index finger spot*

*On the side of the finger nearest the thumb at the base of the nail

Drawing by Ryan Tannascoli - www.ryantannascoli.com

© Callahan Techniques, Ltd. www.RogerCallahan.com

Roger J. Callahan, PhD, used with permission:
www.RogerCallahan.com.

The techniques are so powerful that they were even used to help victims
during the Kosovo War. This following letter was sent from the Kosovo
Medical Battalion Chief of Staff to Roger Callahan.

Richard Cook

TRUPAT E MBROJTJES SË KOSOVËS
SHTABI I PËRGJITHSHËM
BATALIONI 40 I MJEKËSISË

Prishtinë me 01/11/2001
Nr. Prot. 03/2269

DR. ROGER CALLAMAN
CALIFORNIA
UNITED STATES OF AMERICA

Dear Dr. Callahan,

Many well-funded relief organizations have treated the post traumatic stress here in Kosova. Some of our people had limited improvement but Kosova had no major change or real hope until volunteer American Professor Carl Johnson came to help us with the method that you discovered, Thought Field Therapy.

We referred our most difficult trauma patients to the Professor. The success from TFT was 100% for every patient and they are still smiling until this day.

The Professor has been training our medical personnel in your amazing methods of psychotherapy and we are also having success now. Dr. Callahan, Kosova loves Thought Field Therapy.

As Chief of Staff of the Medical Battalion of K.P.C I have full, athority over all medical decisions in Kosova. I am revising this completely and starting a new national program.

The emphasis of the national program will be Thought Field Therapy.

Dr. Shkelzen Syla
Chief of Staff

Roger J. Callahan, PhD, used with permission:
www.RogerCallahan.com.

34

Neuro Linguistic Programming (NLP)

NLP has given me the opportunity to look at my thinking and play with the thoughts and feelings associated with how I viewed 'my arms' and how I now feel: very different ☺ I had become so attached (associated with an issue) that it was having an effect on every area of my life. Changing the thoughts (becoming disassociated) and detaching myself from how I viewed things, changed my life for the better in every area.

I could now start to focus on the things I want in my life: I would redirect my thoughts to be more positive. I would start to feel the positive thoughts being absorbed by my body and then act on these feelings to change my behaviour.

So what is NLP?

NLP provides a way for me to change my thoughts (neuro) by altering the language I use verbally (linguistic) and non-verbally (body language) and re programme (make a new action) to achieve more than I have ever done.

'Get the Life you Want' by Richard Bandler (Co Creator of NLP) gives an insight to how I have changed, by altering thoughts, to get the desired outcome.

NLP has been—and still is—something that I am intrigued by and enjoy learning. Neuro Linguistic Programming is simply giving me a new way of thinking. It's like giving my mind a rewire: no more short circuits such as panic attacks. The feeling from these just kept me stuck: my whole body would clam up, shudder and leave me unable to do anything. NLP has made me realise that much of what I went through was absorbed through my senses. Sight, sound, hearing, feeling and even different tastes; these all became reminders of what I didn't want but I didn't know it consciously. My unconscious did. So over the years I had unknowingly repeated the anxiety, panic attacks and depression over and over again.

Now NLP gives me the means to view things from a more conscious level of thinking and reprogramme my mind with thoughts that belong to a confident person. One of my abilities, as I now recognise, is the one to visualise. Over the years I have been able to look back and almost be in the picture of a particular event, attracting the negative stuff that went with it.

Now I know, having unconsciously learnt the negative stuff, I can turn it around and go the other way. The learned behaviour is there and became an automatic pilot. Now I use my senses to help me to create a better way of life. Sounds that once would put me into a negative frame of mind are simply turned down in volume.

Being relaxed now enables me to feel comfortable in new environments where people are present. Often I would look ahead at things and create a picture in my mind that would get me to move away. This would happen before. I even went into a particular environment, like a coffee shop: once would be a no go, if busy.

So in effect I was always associating a bad childhood feeling and bringing it into adult life. NLP helped me to detach the thoughts of myself and allow me to experience life differently.

Now with NLP I am like an artist, creating pictures in my mind of how I would like my life to look. I focus on these pictures and act them out. I become what I think about: a person who is at peace now. ☺ I certainly was not a few years ago.

Affirmations

Affirmations have become a major part of my life. They have helped in creating what I want. These are simply statements that I have written down to remind me of what I want: I now understand their value in helping me to move forward. Over the years, I have absorbed other people's thoughts of not being able to do certain things. So I was affirming negative thoughts over and over again: no wonder I was getting into such a poor mental state! I was literally telling myself that I couldn't do certain things. Having become aware of this, I got to tell myself a new story. Something that inspires me.

☺ I had now realised I only needed to create thoughts that turned things around, 180 degrees!

So I had to create new thoughts and feelings through affirmations. I consciously chose what I wanted in my life. Setting myself a direction then feeling good about it and acting in accordance with.

The affirmations that I have used are along these lines:

I am whole and perfect just as I am.

I am a calm and tranquil person

I deeply love and accept myself.

Vision board

Something else I use is called a 'vision board'. This is a visual reminder of what I want to bring into my life. That can be health, wealth, relationships or financial goals. It is like a plan but in a visual format. By visualizing what is on the board, I am reminding myself what I want in my life. This somehow keeps me on track with where I am going. It is much like having a five year plan on a board in front of you but made of lots of visual information. It is another tool to bombard my subconscious with new thoughts of what I want to create in my life. Further information can be obtained from www.johnassaraf.com

Visualisation

This is another powerful tool in my set: it has helped me to create this book. Often, at the gym, I would think and visualise my website, my book and what I want to achieve with it. It is a tool that helps me to propel things forward. It also helps in the creative process of things with the book. As with many plans they change, but these plans change to hone in on the goal.

These changes may occur on a daily basis. In some cases, mine did. Now, there are things I want in my life: visualising helps me to bring them into my life. There may be a trigger, may even be a shop sign, a colour or different foods. The trigger from each of these keeps me locked on to my target. The title of the book came from visualising a more successful me. I visualise being a happier person with this physical difference. 'Success in my hands' is a journey not the destination. Whilst I feel at peace I can see all the good coming from it. I can now see myself as out of the box, willing to have a go at whatever I want. I now have thoughts, better feelings and actions going in one direction. All in alignment ☺

Audio mp3's

Personal development audio mp3s have been something that I use every day. They help me with being in a peaceful state of mind. They energise me in ways that I have never known. These audios have a hypnotic effect on what I do: I seem to be acting out what I am listening to.

I have carefully selected the ones that I want: all for self development and moving forward. These help me to create new patterns of thought which allow new and exciting things in my life. I now seem to be generating new circuits within my mind. I now feel I can try something new with feeling good just as I am.

As the new thought patterns are being created, new actions are being taken. I wish I had consciously known this a few years ago, but I had to learn: I had to learn to allow things to come into my life. Over the years, I had resisted everything.

'What resists, persists' seems to be the phrase I recall. Many of the audios can be downloaded from the internet. There is a list of websites for information at the end of the book. They offered me an alternative way of learning. I could now decide what is right for me. Learning my way, slightly different to others, but learning my way gave me the peace of mind: that peace of mind that I had spent nearly a lifetime looking for!

Audio CD's

There are numerous personal development programmes available on CD. I have acquired many of the CD's developed by Michael Neill, Joe Vitalae and Paul Mckenna.

Each of these gives a unique perspective on helping me grow as a human being. I am proud to have taken the opportunity to just learn from them. There is a list of websites at the back of the book: many of the CDs can be purchased from these.

Self Hypnosis

This is much more of a case of deep relaxation: I've tried this a few times and it works wonders. Just being calm is something I never really felt until I started learning and using these tools. I am fascinated by hypnosis. The late Milton Erickson developed 'Erickson Hypnosis '

He had a disability and perhaps that's why there is such a fascination in it. I have always been intrigued with how people deal with things, according to their physical conditions. What techniques do they use on a daily basis? Where did they learn them from? Or, in some cases, did they develop them themselves with the circumstances they were in? For instance, I suppose my obsession was to resolve the thinking.

I guess some will ask how, why etc. For me being relaxed through self hypnosis in social situations gave me a feeling that replaced the anxious one. I could now interact more effectively. Feel good about myself and smile from within. I kind of grew up with a smile that perhaps was masked by what was going on inside. Now the smile within can be seen through others smiling back at me. They somehow know I am at peace. Peace and my own freedom is all that I have been asking for.

Meditation

I am still learning this one. It does calm the mind. I have yet to master it, though. I use it at work on my breaks: sitting and looking out into the farmers fields. There is a landscape that is breathtaking, like a painting on a canvas. I just look at it. Just letting my thoughts flow through me much like the clouds passing by. No judgement, just letting them go by.

I have found energy from doing it, as well. It is a view of farmers' field with hills in the distance. It's a great view. I just look out into the distance and do nothing other than listen to what is going on outside and watch the clouds move across the sky. Talk about a tranquil setting! This peace of mind provides me with a sense of allowing the day to be a good one. A relaxed, enjoyable one.

As you can see, there are many different thought tools available. I have used some in isolation and some in a combination.

Success has come about through using these, day in and day out. The next chapter 'Practice! Practice! Practice!' gives an account of what I do. The tools are available to me now anytime of the day, in any place. I use them before I go to sleep and when I wake up.

The tools provide a foundation for me to continue growing and learning. Late in life, I know. But I feel proud to have taken the time to learn them. I could have had a life full of negative emotions, going nowhere other than on a downward slope of destruction. I knew personally that the peace would come from finding help. Some people say now I am too calm ☺ but at least I have my peace of mind. ☺ Calmness comes with it.

What has TFT done for me?

TFT has given me a tool to 2 calm myself.

I feel at peace in various social situations. Since using the technique, I managed to get hold of a job and there has been not one day off due to sickness, so far. To me that's remarkable. Over the years, the low self esteem, anxiety and depression, kept me from being able to work. Now I am working with people with cerebral palsy who have a range of other disabilities. Due to my poor thinking, I was too busy trying to fit in. It didn't work. Jobs were short lived. Either asked to leave or I left on my own accord.

TFT has helped in eliminating the blocks I have in my mind and enabling me to move forward. Forward thinking is ever present and those thoughts are maintained day in day out. A new programme as it were for my mind is being installed. TFT removes the old one: I now decide consciously what I want and who I am and act upon it. Erasing the 'dis' out of disability and creating a person with a UNIQUE ABILITY. Realising that, each thought, now and in my future, will bring a happier and more peaceful Richard.

As time goes by, the old patterns of holding myself back are becoming less and less, as I use the tools to get back to the real me. Whole and perfect just as I am ☺

Through using TFT, there is a feeling of empowerment that has come from taking responsibility for my own personal growth. I had been in what I called a 'victim mentality' for many years. This mentality had come from years of social conditioning: of course it was not my fault but now it is my responsibility to change.

Empowerment gives me a choice: it enables me to think of what I want, to choose was is right for me. Having the ability to say no to certain things that will certainly send me back to the old pattern of thinking. The empowerment process now gives me the opportunity to choose. To choose to give back what I have learnt so that more good can be done.

How is NLP helping me?

NLP is a tool that helps with creating something new for me. It helps with taking me from where I am at now to where I want to be. I imagine myself as a more confident person. I use the environment to help me with moving forward. For instance: visualising myself being taller than the buildings as I walk down the street creates confidence. NLP helps with the fact I feel I am driving a car that has the brakes off: I now can steer it in the direction I want. With this tool that I have I can alter, change the inner and visualise a better me. Using my senses, instead of being used by them, creating havoc in my life.

Creww repeating affirmations

Affirmations with a set direction of where I want to go in my life have moved me forward. These are formed through feeling a sense of purpose, passion and with a feeling of what I want happening now.

An example of mine.

I deeply accept myself as being whole and perfect just as I am: this has enabled me to live freely with an acceptance of myself.

'I love my arms just as they are'

'I feel at peace with who I am each and everyday.'

Using a Vision board

The vision board is yet another tool for keep my mind on track, on track with where I want to go. It forms a visual reminder of my goals. Each day I remind myself of what is ahead now. Photos, places I want to visit, fundraising and other goals are all placed to form a map of my future. My map, my direction, my route to get what I deserve in my life. The board in essence could be viewed much like watching a play. I decide what characters are in it. All the lights used to show the characters in the play all point towards the stage: without those lights I cannot see the play and I miss out!

Visualisation.

Visualisation helps me move forward to where I am going. Without that picture in my mind then I would probably stray off course, away from the goals. Visualisation helps with keeping me on track. A track that leads to the goals I have in mind. This is a powerful tool to use. It is also a starting point for seeing a dream become a reality. It is also a tool to see where I want to be in a few years time.

Audio mps and CDs

Self development programmes contained in mps are my music of choice. At the back of the book, I have listed the sites where I have obtained them. Many have had a place in me moving forward. I have also listened to some cds by some of the authors listed at the back of the book. They all help to keep me in a peaceful frame of mind that I am now accustomed to.

Self hypnosis

Hypnosis has helped me to stay in a tranquil state of mind. An Erickson hypnosis course being my introduction to it. It helps with allowing myself more time to interact with people and accelerate the desire outcome that I am looking for. Relaxation has accelerated my learning. Even with the qualifications that I do have, they took longer to gain due to heighted states of anxiety. As the months and years roll forward, I am becoming more relaxed. The more relaxed I am, the more I seem to learn. With this start of mind I also feel more creative and act on the ideas easily and effortlessly.

Meditation

Being still in mind, to me has felt like a miracle. 30 or so years ago, I was with a mind full of a negative self talk: now with a stillness that is like a calm sea. Meditation with more practice provides a calm ocean for me. I thoroughly recommend at least trying it even for short periods of time. Even at work I allow a few minutes where a view provides a stillness for me. Some meditation mps are also included in the back of the book to help if needed.

So have the tools helped?

A definite yes is the answer to that question. How did I know they were the right tools for me? To be honest, a gut feeling at first. I had listened for many years to others: I am grateful for their advice and time. Yet I felt I had to find the answer within me. That answer has always been there. I just needed to ask myself the right questions. Following my heart instead of my head. So by following my heart and only knowing it was the right route to take led me to learning all these tools. I am still learning and always will. But I am eternally grateful for getting back my peace of mind.

With the tools that I now have I feel I can step into the unknown much more easily. There is a sense to keep going, no matter what! If a path leads to a dead end, I look at it and learn something from it. A dead end gives me time to stop, look and listen. To turn around and see the same path from a different perspective. Hopefully the steps I took can help others. The tools are there and they are there to help ourselves with helping others.

> *'It is one of the most beautiful compensations of this life*
> *that no man can sincerely try to help another without*
> *helping himself . . . . serve and thou shall be served'*
> **Ralph Waldo Emerson.**

Chapter 3
Practice! Practice! Practice!

Ask yourself the secret of your success. Listen to your answer,
and practice it.

Richard Bach

After so many years spent looking, I finally found what I was looking for. The tools that were given to me worked. ☺ So each day I keep practicing using the tools for my mind. At first there were a few mistakes or feedback. It was obvious to me that it would take some time to learn them. But I just needed to practice. It is like being a sportsman: you only get better with practice. The talent may be there. But is has to be harnessed one way or another.

'My secret is practice'
Beckham, David

Having realised I had perhaps acquired a great way of attracting negative stuff through my thinking, I could now somehow attract the positive stuff into my life. One thought at a time. But I needed to practice.

Some would say where would you find the time? So whenever and wherever I could, I would. How did I practice with these new tools?

- Whilst walking down the street listening to the mp3's with self help info and guided meditations.
- At work when I know my energy levels have dropped. TFT would be used.
- By reading a book over coffee. Most people know me as a keen coffee drinker. ☺ Much of my learning has been through relaxing with a book.
- Writing new affirmations for the goals I want to achieve. The affirmations have to be in alignment with the direction I want to go.
- Adding more pictures on my vision board to keep the overall goal in mind.
- Visualising being a more confident and happier person walking down the street.
- Changing the language I use about my hands, from saying it is a disability to one where I see them as unique and a part of the whole of me. A new enabled way of thinking that works for me.

I would at least use some of the tools to ensure I had a good day! Now I feel that, if my day starts well, then the rest of the day will be fine. I work with feeling good wherever and whenever. Thirty years of 'not so good' to me is a very long time. So no wonder I wanted a change. Now I know how. Practicing with the tools gave me the means to change. A chance to change as well.

> *'Practice means to perform, over and over again in the face of all obstacles, some act of vision, of faith, of desire. Practice is a means of inviting the perfection desired'*
>
> **Martha Graham**

For many years I had practiced a way of thinking that, obviously, did not work.

> *"If you do what you've always done, you'll get what you've always gotten."*
>
> **Antony Robbins**

So many things in my life were not working: I was always thinking the same and getting the same.

So what would I have to do now to change all of that? Firstly I would have to think differently. Well that was something I had never done before.

How would I know it would work? Well the old pattern of thinking, which to me I had perfected, made me feel bad. So, with thinking the opposite of what I had been thinking, would I feel good?

Well the answer to that is a BIG YES! My life has transformed. I feel happier, healthier and in control of my life. So how have I done this? Since 2006 I have practiced, practiced and practiced using the tools for my mind every single day.

Exercising my mind. We go to the gym to get fit physically and, as a result, we actually feel better. I like to feel better now through thinking better thoughts about myself so that I can go to the gym.

The workout to me consists of reading, listening to audio tapes and rehearsing what I want in my life. Changing my thoughts to change my life! Thoughts that DIS ABLE do exactly that. Thoughts that EN ABLE do the same. I have chosen the latter! But I had to practice, practice and practice.

So where and when would I practice using the tools? Well, each morning I would get up and use the TFT techniques that I now have become so familiar with. My days now start off with much more energy than I had a few years ago: friends and family saw what I was like. Now I am glad to say I am much more at peace now and I am sure that is what they wanted for me! The TFT: I still am astounded with.

I use it every day and now I have a coach who is helping me to direct my thinking to where I want to go in my life. The road blocks that I had a few years ago have finally gone. I feel that I can go anywhere with my life now. Choose what I want to do and be carefree enough to enjoy life by being Richard rather than trying to be like others. That's empowering and, to be honest, that's who I wanted to be. Just to be myself. No anxiety, no depression, no panic attacks and no reason to fuel self sabotaging behaviour.

Why would I want to hold onto old patterns of thought that didn't work? Makes little sense to me now that I am aware of what I was thinking. So where and when would I practice using these tools?

I have already mentioned first thing in the morning with TFT. Other examples have been at the gym. Mentally rehearsing what I want to do. Thinking of chapter names, what to include and what would inspire me to keep writing. 'Success in my hands' is an inspiring thought for me. I always wanted an end to that way of thinking that had limited me so much. So whilst on a bike, I focus on the name and how good it makes me feel.

Visualising my website, with blogs, photos and challenges for fundraising: new ideas and new ways of improving who I am, provides direction to the website. Do I need to sit down in a room and brainstorm when ideas are flowing through my mind when getting fit? Also thinking of it differently, creating a fitter me and developing new ideas. That seems to sound just as good.

Audio Cd's and mp3's have become a great part of my life. The likes of Michael Neil, Joe Vitale and many self hypnosis mp3 downloads have been a blessing for me. The stories and knowledge within has enriched my life. Paul Mckennas Cd'S and books are also on my collection list. TFT and Hypnosis courses through Kevin Laye so far have been instrumental in gaining more knowledge for me to perform better.

Neuro Linguistic Programming or NLP is an area I am working on. Thinking differently has come about by creating new patterns of thought. Old patterns made me unhappy. The new patterns are uplifting and help me perform better. I now look at feeling great all the time: so much of my thinking is devoted to do what is working.

It seems like I am redesigning my mind to work effectively. It is like saying why design a bridge to fail: we always look at designing for a bridge to withstand as much as nature can throw at it. That is what I am doing now! I have been lucky to have found myself again. I feel proud and humbled by the journey. Books by Richard Bandler give a bigger picture of what NLP can do. I am fascinated by my own thinking and how it can be changed in an instant.

I seem to respond well to positive thinking , especially that of my own making. Many years ago I felt the full force of being different. I could not work out why people would look and ask questions in a certain way that would lead me to feeling bad. Now I understand that—with practicing the tools I have been given—I can let other people's negative views or looks wash over me.

Anything negative that comes from someone else seems to bounce off me now. I only allow positive things to flow into my life. Allow being positive on the inside seems to reflect a positivity on the outside.

Visualisation has a massive impact on where I want to be. Many athletes use this tool and it is definitely an extremely powerful one. Visualisation gives me the opportunity to view things as if they are already happening NOW! Yet this may be a goal a couple of years away. I talked about this book few years ago: somehow it is now materialising. I needed to grow in between to become someone different. Pardon the pun. ☺

But who I was some time ago, compared to the person I am now, is a world apart. Yet now I am happier and calmer within which is allowing my writing to flow and give you and insight of my thinking.

In the past, even if I could visualise what I wanted I would sabotage my dreams through inappropriate thinking. Now with my intentions in mind, I feel with the right thinking patterns that I can achieve them. It is like I have shifted a mind-set to help me with the visualisation process. My goals are in my mind daily now.

Pictures on a vision board help me to keep on track each day. Every time I look at the board I know all will be ok and that my dreams will happen as I stay on the path to creating what I want.

I suppose one incredible aspect of my journey is that, although it took 25 to 30 years to obtain peace, it was worth it. It shows that , where there are challenges that seem impossible, the mind has a way of creating the possible if we chose to do so. A way was found for me. 25-30 years ago, I did not simply say to myself TFT, NLP and hypnosis would be the secret for me, although these were already around. I just was not aware then. Now having experienced many journeys along many different paths, I was actually finding my way to a new destination.

That destination was my own peace and freedom for myself with the physical difference I have. If I had visualised that, with a thinking pattern on track with it, then the peace would have come sooner!

So what else adds as a guide to where I now want to go? Other tools include using affirmations. I practice these daily, sometimes hourly, depending on what I am feeling. The affirmations are really my thoughts written down with a feeling as if they are happening now.

Many of the self help books give a great guide on what affirmations can do for you. If you think 'you can' or think 'you can't' either way you are affirming to yourself what you can and cannot do. I was no different.

I had negative thoughts that I somehow affirmed over and over again. And guess what, what I was thinking literally became true. 'Not wanting to go out because of being different' has changed to 'going out because I can.' The feeling of difference has gone. I am confident and self-assured: this is my affirmation. Hey presto self-assurance and confident is how I am feeling. What a turnaround and a great feeling to have.

By practicing my new way of thinking, a new life seems to be unfolding.

A life full of being in flow. No more road blocks, no more setbacks that allow me to put a halt on my direction in life. Practicing gives way to do such things automatically after a while: the auto pilot is now on course for success.

The auto pilot that I had before was always on self-destruct: now the auto pilot button is pressed for achieving all that I want in life. But, in all of this, I decide where I want to go.

I also read different self-help books which teach me new things. I have found them invaluable in my learning. Many of these authors have lived and breathed through extremely difficult times. But one thing seems to be showing up all the time: their achievements are made through a way of thinking. Success has come about through thinking the right way, following through with the right action and with a self-assurance to keep going, no matter what.

'Success in my hands' has come about in the same way. Ironically, it is still about a way of thinking. The thinking now incorporates all the tools techniques and examples I learned from others. 'Success in my hands' is about doing such things: practice, practice and practicing. Whilst these things may have not been in a particular rational order, the success has come about through doing that.

It didn't just appear overnight. I had to work as much as I could to get to where I am now. Victory over myself, I suppose. I always had a belief I would get there one day: I just didn't know when. I seem more proactive about doing things. I seem to be in alignment with what I want. My body and mind going in the same direction: it is a fantastic feeling.

The disability has disappeared from my mind, giving space to one of unique ability. I prefer to use empowering words. Ones that enable me to do so much more. Positive language gives positive results. The results speak for themselves. They are the true measurement for success. 'Success in my hands is a result! A journey that has taken a long time but nevertheless a result. I personally believe others can achieve significant changes in thinking over a shorter space of time by taking a leap of faith and using these tools. I changed more in 5 years than I ever changed in nearly 30. That's testament to the power of the mind and the tools that are available to help.

The TFT, after a while, becomes an unconscious tool that is always at hand. At first, the practicing side of things was something I felt out of my comfort zone. I had been so comfortable with the old way of thinking that the new one would take time to sink in.

So how was the line crossed to help me move forward. Well in one word . . . TRUST! I had found that TFT worked and I trusted it. The trust came from the change in the feelings I experienced. The change in my expression: a better feeling and the smile would return.:)

My testimonial provides my reasoning for using TFT and some of the other tools. Now with an awareness of my own thinking I can develop a new pattern of thought and practice it, practice it and practice it until it becomes automatic. This creates a new set of beliefs and actions from which I start to create a better life for myself. I feel as if, by practicing, I have gone from disabling myself to enabling myself. All through my thinking.

Success is much about the journey rather than the final result. The journey even to me is inspiring. How have I done it? How could I have turned my thinking around? Also what does this new thinking do for me and those around me? It's like my own reality has completely changed.

I am always listening to audios and CDs. Now I have a fascination with my own thinking and perhaps how is the best to think. Thoughts seem to have an amazing effect on my personal well-being. The audios and CDs that I listen to are about changing my own subconscious to enable me to align with the goals I have in mind. Audios help to remove unconscious blocks that may slow down my improvement. Some are hypnotic in nature, others help me think laterally. Pretty much opening my mind to allow things to happen, rather than having a closed mind and resisting change.

NLP helps me with creating new learning patterns and then creating new ways of living my life. New thoughts of a positive nature produce good feeling from which I go and act on. The action seems to be more in flow. No holding back but a calm self assurance that all will be ok. I seem to be more playful with my thinking. I guess that comes from once being a child. Free thinking: the playfulness is with my imagination. I write down all the ideas that come to my mind.

The NLP allows me to use my imagination as a means for moving forward. Instead of being stuck in a pattern of thought that limits my potential.

As I have changed my thinking , new things are starting to happen. Better thoughts create better experiences. Through these experiences, I am fully aware of how I feel now: energised, vitalised and with a clarity of mind I have never experienced before. It seems that I can remain in the present moment longer than I have ever been in my life time.

Being in the now is a precious present: no anxiety from my past and no concerns for my future. Now I am what I experience and, perhaps, that is why I am so happy.

So NOW is a focus of my life. I have even thought that, by rearranging the word NOW and spelling it backwards, it spells WON. Perhaps focusing on the now I have won. Won a battle of my own mind for most of my life.

That battle was trying to find peace. But peace was already there: I just had to find a way to allow it back into my life. I had learned to fight over the years. Yet, by allowing and forgiving all that has gone on in the past, the peace in the NOW has arrived. Everything that I allow with a clear, calm and self-assured state of mind, will appear much faster.

Visualisation is part of what I practice in order to see my dream come into my life. There is something about the power of now: seeing my dream being created in my mind now is something that I have never been able to do. The pictures I had in mind were all over the place: everything seemed inconsistent with what I wanted. Yet now, with seeing my life as completely the opposite, the results are more in alignment. The alignment has come through using the tools and changing my beliefs so that my life goes in the right direction.

The awareness of my own thoughts now is far greater than it used to be. I am free to be myself, now. I don't feel the need to fit in, anymore. I like to be in a world where I can make it happen for me: my reality being created rather than just being a part in everyone else's.

It feels like, by practicing each day, I am creating not just a new me but a new improved world around me. By practicing the tools for my mind, I become the best I can be. But, as I find new tools to use, I become better and better. Something that, after 40 years, is astounding.

The affirmations form part of the focus for delivering what I want in my life: I have written down many of them over the last year or so. Then I have specifically chosen ones that I believe to be right for me. The feeling now comes from loving who I am as a whole person and being perfect as I am. Why would I want to change the very essence of me to fit in with others? I am ME. So my affirmations reflect that. Affirmations, stated in the positive with feeling as if they are happening NOW, are awesome. They work. I know they work because I experienced the negative side of affirming things to myself for far too long.

Success now is more about the journey. I have been able to turn my thinking around literally 180 degrees. From negative to positive. Success started many years ago but I just didn't know how to change. I was always looking for help especially at school: as a teenager I knew what thoughts I wanted to change.

My attitude was to find a way, no matter what: never quit but find an alternative if something was not working. So in hindsight I was practicing to succeed, although I consciously didn't know it. Now with the turnaround and with the right tools I can practice and succeed in every area of my life. Forward thinking with a clear mind brings my dreams closer to becoming a reality.

So how did practicing help me?

By practicing using the tools there comes freedom.

Freedom to express who I am. I am at peace. Peace with who I am with the body I have. I feel whole and perfect just as I am. The tools I have been given and learnt to use through everyday practice, have given me the sense of purpose that I feel I came into this world for. I only wanted to be me, instead of trying to fit in a world where I took onboard other people thoughts and feelings of how I look.

Practicing each day now has become much like driving a car. First gear: mind whizzing so fast going slowly. Gear two: mind slowing down a little but getting there a little quicker. Gear three, gear four and gear five: mind moving economically and getting so much done. Now there is a thought! ☺

Practicing using the tools enabled me to follow my heart.

I feel like a bee buzzing around collecting nectar, using the energy provided to create something through my thoughts, feelings and actions. I love who I am now. The very essence of who I am keeps me going. Whilst I am different, the difference now gives me the opportunity to help others to be themselves and create what they want out of their own lives.

Practicing has allowed me to change.

It is evident that the same thought pattern held me back for so many years. Now with practicing using a variety of tools, I can change. Be better than I used to be. I can start to create rather than destroy. I feel the change is not only better for me but I can see it in those around me. Family and friends seem different towards me as the changes have occurred. More smiles, more positivity and life seems to feel good. Without practicing none of this would have happened.

Chapter 4
Disabling to enabling

*'Desire is the key to motivation, but it's determination and commitment to an unrelenting pursuit of your goal—a commitment to excellence—that will **enable** you to attain the success you seek'*

Mario Andretti
Italian born American Race driver

I went from disabling to **enabling** by changing my thoughts day after day. Change your thoughts and you can change your life! 'Success in my hands' has been—in essence—just that!

I had to change my thinking to take me from disabling to enabling. I had spent too many years with self-defeating patterns of thinking. Everything I wanted in my life seemed to slip between my fingers.

I felt I had no control until now. What I had to do was change my way of thinking, let go of the past. The past now has no control over me. I had to create a new me. I can now set my own compass to achieve what I set out to do: the physical difference now is a part of the whole me.

My thoughts of the past were thoughts that disabled me! It shows that, what we think about, we become. The effect from that thinking led me to limit myself. I wanted to do so much but my past held me back.I allowed it to hold me back: every time I tried to move forward with my wants and needs my old thinking patterns kept me anchored to the past.

I hope that my story gives people the opportunity to help themselves much like I have. I spent nearly half of my life disabling myself: now the rest is dedicated to enable myself.

Changing the way I thought about myself through different levels of thinking led me to change. TFT not only unlocked a door to a new life but it allowed me to walk through it.

Changing the way I think also has changed the way I see my world. It seems that my life has been like a mirror: disabling negative thoughts created disabling negative experiences. For example debt, challenges with alcohol, poor relationships and little employment.

Changing my thoughts is empowering and enabling: I only learned to be a disabled person through the language that was spoken to me. It disempowered me. I wanted to be just me. Me with the physical difference, yet happy with it.

Now 30 plus years later I am. Just proud to be me, although this journey has been a long one. I am grateful of the journey. I somehow feel energised through finally finding my own peace, with all the help that has been given to me.

It may seem like I have been a dormant volcano waiting to erupt. Having been dormant for years I NOW feel that there is so much positive energy to be unleashed: nothing will stop me. Volcanoes cannot be stopped once they erupt. But when they do stop and the lava stops flowing, new life begins. I see that in me now.

I have lived on islands and seen what there is to offer. May be part of me still views life from an island perspective. Back to nature as it were: nature seems to have a way of finding its own equilibrium.

Now I have found my own equilibrium through a way of thinking. Removing negative destructive patterns of thought, generating new thoughts that create a new happier me. It does feel like nature's medicine has helped in a way.

The journey from disabling to enabling may seem long but the changes have happened for the better in a short space of time. I NOW empower myself with choosing thoughts that make me feel good. I choose thoughts that create stepping stones instead of looking at barriers to overcome. Barriers are something we try to break down, get over, around or underground. I just like to place stepping stones in front of me, choosing the direction I want to go with each new stone.

It seems that focusing away from the so called disability and creating a new person who is unique in his own way has given me a choice. A choice to either carry on with the old way of thinking—which disempowers—or start to create new thoughts that empower. The empowerment process has been my way forward as well as a healthier one.

With the empowering way of thinking where do you think I can go? First of all forward! I feel energised through feeling at peace with myself: I get to do more. See more and feel more good feelings. ☺

Those feelings can then be used as a means to stepping into the new. Stepping in to the new with good feelings, gives me confidence to achieve more. A sense of ease and a knowing that all will be ok with whatever I will do.

To enable myself to do what I want has taken practice: each day I mentally ensure that I am on track. I have written things down, instead of thinking the old way of thinking, and then just remembering them.

Writing things down has been part of the strategy for enabling. It reinforces my desires of what I want in my life. It focuses my mind on the intentions and keeps me going in the direction I want. I have written on A2 paper my intentions and what I am feeling with regards to them.

I have also two mentors to help me with enabling myself to move forward: they are both unique and have their own amazing abilities in helping people. They help in creating what I want to achieve and I am grateful to them. I guess the key was to take charge of my own life and let go of the past. There has also been a sense of surrendering to it. Holding my hands up and saying to myself: I choose peace over this. I had to find a way!

Focusing on my physical difference was disabling me and I had been fighting for so many years against that. Focusing on what I wanted out of life with passion and feeling is my way forward. Resonating from within, changing my deep inner thoughts to create a better world for myself. Attracting all the positive things life has to offer.

When I started to think positively at a subconscious level, I started to see positive outcomes in my outer world as it were. People smile more and they react in a positive way. It seems so much easier now than it did a few years ago. It is like I have turned a tap on and clean, life-giving water is flowing out. How could this possibly be? I still have to pinch myself, from time to time. This transformation seems unbelievable yet somehow it's true.

The title of the book was chosen that way. 'Success in my hands' is my way of saying that I have done it. In the past, I allowed my old thinking to give me failures or negative feedback. Now the feedback is success: I now look at my hands as being a part of the whole. A unique part of me, instead of associating my hands as being something I don't like. More positive thoughts at a deeper level have brought about a sense of ease at the surface: everybody can see it.

> *'Once you replace negative thoughts with positive ones,*
> *you' ll start having positive results'.*
> **Willie Nelson**

Disabling to enabling is a journey that I have been on and, perhaps, I still am and likely to be for the rest of my life. It has taken many different paths but now there is no path to take if I am myself.

Over the years, the challenge for me has been getting out there and letting go of my fears of others and how they view me. Now there is a sense of being empowered with the help from others. All I did was to keep asking for help with a knowing that the right support would turn up one day. I still needed the help from another person: they did help me but I did it my way! With the tears in my eyes now the smile comes from within. Yep, I bloody well did it my way and I knew I could.

As Kevin Laye wrote in the foreword. 'He did it, because he knew he could'

Now I do it because I am . . . 'ME' ☺

Disabling to enabling is much about my learning to enable myself. No one else did it for me: I didn't just wake up one morning to find all my fears and anxieties gone. It has taken the best part of 5-6 years. Using TFT each day , creating new patterns of thinking to move me forward and keep me on track. Tapping created more time. The reason I say that is that much of my time was absorbed by thinking thoughts that disabled me. TFT gave me the time to be free with my thoughts. To decide what I want to do in an instant.

But what I do NOW is recognise my thoughts: waking up in the morning feeling good ☺ Feeling good or great in the morning gives rise to the day being good or great. The old associations of how I look have disappeared. Long gone are the days of waking up and not wanting to go out.

Now I feel care-free, with no attachment to my arms. I can do anything I put my mind to and, sure enough, I will. The willpower is there, the resilience has always been there. It was always going to be me that had the power to change: what a GREAT feeling to have.

As a kid, I consciously recognised I was different. I must have been carefree. That very essence of just being and doing without a care in the world. Kids seem to just live in the NOW before life throws stuff in their way. They do things that adults would never dream of doing without judging first: I am no different to that. I was once carefree and NOW I am hoping to be much more of that. That's how I may be able to live a more fulfilling life. Caring, yes, but letting go of being too attached to something to make it happen. But just with a sense that, if I believe that it can be done, it will and a way will be found. I have already done it with the association around my arms.

Now I can laugh and joke about them. Also I smile much more when people ask. That in itself eases others to continue with asking more questions. You see disabling to enabling is much more than it seems: while I can do more, I communicate more. This communication creates enabling situations. I use spoken words that help me, keeping me moving forward to achieving my dreams ☺

That sense of feeling good about myself enables me. It creates a vibrational bubble of good feelings, so to speak. Feeling good rubs off on others, whether I have short arms or not. So it seems by looking at my thinking. I just had poor thinking.

While working on developing new ideas to enable me to do more, I think NOW of being comfortable with who I am. This feeling of ease and happiness seems to allow more to come into my life. There is a new me now who I intend to keep by being free ☺

Along with this, a sense of allowing things to flow in and out of my life comes. If I get stuck, I know what to do to give myself a nudge in the right direction.

To help with the nudge I write things down, use TFT, self-hypnosis and read the books that are included at the end. Those books form a part of my progress. I have been intrigued with my own thinking. How could I have gone so long in the wrong direction?

Yet I feel at peace with it as I know now that the paradox was what wasn't working was perhaps working. Some people discover things in a short space of time: I guess I just took a little longer. But in the space of time for my new way of thinking 5 to 6 years to turn around 25 to 30 years of inappropriate thinking is time well spent. The tools to enable have been around for years: I just needed to connect with them. It's like being on a frequency that gives you just static. But when I tuned into something that gave me more good feelings, I wanted to stay on that frequency. Staying tuned!

So does the fact that I have short arms make a difference? I say NO. My thoughts are based upon wanting good feelings. So, by concentrating on these, I get more of the same. 'You always get more of what you focus on' springs to mind as I write this. How true. What I thought of more than five years ago led to a destructive lifestyle.

Now my thoughts lead to a constructive and creative lifestyle. I guess it's much like creating a building. Build a strong foundation and the building lasts for a very long time. Build a foundation that cannot hold the weight of life above it and what happens? It fails. I was going that way, somehow. Now for the rest of my life I am building a new foundation. Reinforcing it as I change and learn more.

At the moment, there is harmony in my life, surrounding every area. I work on each area with a coach who helps me to achieve what I want out of my life. The old childish me is now supported by an adult with a greater knowledge of life. The child in me was scared as he became more aware of his surroundings. Yet to change I now allow the adult to look back and see what the child in me would have wanted.

The support he would have liked. The friends that he would have liked to have been with. The adult NOW merges with this inner child, looking at all his situations NOW and where he felt slightly uncomfortable. So now

I take the time to consider what the child in me would want while the adult enjoys his life like he has been given a second chance. What he has done is take command over his life, whereas before the child would be the reason for his challenges.

The adult becomes someone new. He acts in the NOW. He thinks in the ways that will help him. He feels the right feelings. Good feelings, loving feelings, feelings of excitement. He also acts in the right way to become an enabled person.

So the thoughts had to change to create the life I would want. Instead of thoughts coming from a victim mentality, I would now find thoughts from a place of empowerment. These thoughts would give me a sense of purpose, a direction with my life that leaves the past behind.

With the tools that are now available to me, I can set my own compass to where I want to go by:

Using the right key

With any lock you have to find the right key or combination and, once you open the door to something new, you surrender to it all. Letting go and living life by being myself: I had to view things from a different perspective. The way I was thinking was not going to give me results in a world that offers so much more: I had to find the right key or tool for me to view things differently. The key to help me think clearer. TFT has enabled me to do that, along with other tools. As I write this I now know TFT has been the key to unlock the door of my own self, the self where I am free. I now make decisions from my heart instead of my head. To come from a place of peace is what I have been looking for. It has arrived and it has enabled me.

Creating intention triggers.

One of the most important things I have to do is keep on track with where I want to go. So I have what I call 'intention triggers'. These may be simple things like writing a note as soon as I have thought of an idea. A post it note put in a strategic place to remind me of my direction, saying no to things that are not on my intention list, reading the right books and stay away from reading newspapers and other material that is not in line of what I want to be.

Happier thoughts create happier circumstances.

For some reason, I feel as if a new life is coming from all the pain and mental turmoil I had. A life worth living and a life worth giving something back. Giving is something I have learnt to do, over the time. I guess before, by not giving, I stayed where I was. I was a person who hid away because he could not confront his fears. Having confronted his fears a new world opens up. What seems to appear is a loving world. Happier thoughts seem to be creating happier circumstances. ☺

Replacing negative thoughts with positive thoughts.

Over and over and over again. I have kept going: new self-empowering thoughts replace the old disempowering ones. A positive one knocking the hell out of the negative one until it disappears. Perhaps now there is a sense of finally loving myself for who I am. This awesome feeling seems to generate such overwhelming results that even I ask the 'how and why is it happening' question.

The answer is that I deserve to be free and at peace with my physical body. Loving it allows for more of the same to come into my life. Enabling things to happen by feeling a certain way: feeling great is fantastic. At last a ray of sunshine seems to be on me all the time. All the good comes from thinking one good thought at a time. Each good thought bringing with it a better feeling. Changing ME from one who allowed disabling thoughts about the arms to somebody who thinks enabling thoughts and almost forgetting that they are how they are. A great feeling of being care-free about them.

Releasing the resistance to change.

By releasing the resistance to change. I am allowing more to come into my life. I am creating the path of least resistance to get to the goal. I have done the hard word, the disabling work and—boy—it was hard! It is like the life being sucked out of you. The easier route is the best. Where the road blocks have been removed from my mind, enabling thoughts seem to have brought a sense of clarity. My mind feels free from all the stress that I have had over the years: I sometimes find myself in awe of this clarity. It feels wonderful. A sense of peace is here to stay. I feel I can now decide what I want to do with lucidity and that will probably appear faster than it has ever done before.

Disabling to enabling, crying to laughing, fearing to loving.

All these words have had an effect on me and on those around me. My world, my thoughts, my feelings and my actions. Well, loving and being grateful for being me seem like a precious present, at last. This precious present now lives a life very much moment by moment. I feel joyful for finally finding my peace and freedom that was covered over by a cloak of fearful thoughts. The cloak has now been removed and the authentic me has been revealed. I am Richard and unique just as everyone else is in their own way.

The latter leading to just being myself. A human being at peace with himself. The journey seems to have felt more than a thousand miles. Yet that journey started with a single step. That step was an intention to find an answer. Using my imagination to find the answer in a different way. The resilience to keep going no matter what. The patience to know that it would arrive at the right time. Each of these took me from disabling myself to enabling myself to be the person I wanted to be. Free to be me ☺

Disabling to enabling has taken me on a journey of finding my true self. That self seems to be one of kindness, happiness, love and gratitude.

Everything seems to happen when these thoughts flow through me rather than resisting change because of how I look and what I thought of as a child. Being in flow much like a river, flowing naturally.

> *God authors desires in your heart, then fulfils his will*
> *by enabling you to realize those desires.*
> **Edwin Louis Cole**

Approximately thirty years later, those desires have been fulfilled! ☺

Chapter 5
I did it my way!

"You've got a song you're singing from your gut, you want that audience to feel it in their gut. And you've got to make them think that you're one of them sitting out there with them too. They've got to be able to relate to what you are doing"

Johnny Cash 1932-2003

So where did the 'I did it my way' start? Well, looking back it all started in my early teens where I wanted to ask questions. I had an overwhelming desire to get answers to feel at peace with my arms however I, perhaps, allowed this obsession to cloud other areas of my life.

That obsession closed doors but, paradoxically, I suppose that it was meant to be. This obsession was kind of working for me: it kept me safe, in one respect. Yet, as I opened up my mind allowing new things and new ideas in my life, I have realised that the obsession had become a brake in my life. A brake that was always on.

I was trying to drive a car with the handbrake on! That really was me in a nutshell. Now, with the handbrake finally off, there is the 'va va voom' in my life. ☺ From doing it my way I seem to feel at ease with everything. I want to learn more from the people who have helped me. I am more open minded about how we think and feel and the actions we take because of those thoughts and feelings.

'I did it my way' is, in one way, a victory over myself. A way of thinking looks like the theme that runs through this movie that has lasted 25 years or so. The theme now is still a way of thinking. But this new movie has a happy person in it.: me

Having done it my way, I found what I was looking for instead of being told what to do from other people. I went along the route of counselling, medication and visits to the gp and even a psychiatrist.

Did it work? Well, it only gave me the desire to work it out for myself. I could have been on anti-depressants for years. And I could definitely have drunk myself to an early grave! Yet, above the clouds, the sun always shines. Something kept telling me I would get there, in the end. I kept saying to people 'I'm getting there.' Sure enough, I have got there, my way!

'I did it my way' has given me the opportunity to see things from a different perspective. I realised that much of what happened was probably not my fault but it was definitely my responsibility to find a way, rather than just sit back and hope that all would come to me. That would have been a shame if I had done nothing.

The learning process has been inspiring for me: it has been challenging. But like most mountains that are there, they are there to be conquered. Whoever conquered them, gave back to the world something of himself, by doing it.

But to overcome those challenges by myself, with the support I chose, is one that is humbling to say the least. Believing in myself was one of the biggest mind-sets I had to have. To know that I would finally find my peace and freedom with my thinking is something I feel even now astounded by.

I sometimes just don't get it. How could I have turned it all around? How could I have changed my beliefs in such a short space of time? Sometimes it doesn't make sense. Some of it is still a bit confusing. Yet that confusion is only a state of mind before things get clear: through that lucidity I can do better things with my life by doing it my way. With a mind-set clear from the emotions of my past. I can set a new direction for my life knowing that, with all my knowledge and experience, I can set new intentions to help others. The same as they helped me.

I suppose by doing it my way I have given myself a new skill. A skill that allows me to explore every avenue to get to where I want to go, with a knowing that I will get the result I intended. To never give in. To look at things and to view things as feedback rather than failure. The paths I took are all feedbacks. The most important feedback now is to be who I am rather than trying to fit in. I was always trying to fit in yet I didn't know how.

The difference I guess was that I felt separate from everyone: I had never met anyone similar to me until I was 28. But now, when I look at the people around me, I know that they had already accepted me for who I am. I just needed to recognise it and accept myself as a whole person.

Now with the tools for my mind and other techniques I have found easy to accept me for me. I am Richard with different arms. I feel great with them now. They are a part of me: a part that I love and cherish. I do feel whole.

That wholeness has come from within, seeing me for who I am and just accepting myself as Richard in a society that, in essence, is looking for the same: accept me for who I am.

Doing this my way has given me the opportunity to look at my own language, the language that I now use. Rather than using the word disability, which being honest I sometimes slip up and use, I prefer to be myself, Richard. Just Me. Unique in my own way, just like everyone else. My journey of learning has given me the ability to turn it around 180 degrees and live the rest of my life as I intend. Being at peace and free with who I am.

The 'doing it my way' for me was part of my dream to feel free of my old thoughts. I'd rarely say to anyone 'What do you think about the route that I am taking to get things resolved?' I just went off and did it! That were my life and my mind, the two most important aspects of me!

No one else could go through this for me. Yet somehow everyone else was part of this journey. I never intended for them to be a part of it: they were just there almost by default. But as I look ahead now, I can start to guide my thoughts to enable me to do what I want.

Thoughts, feelings and actions are described in the book 'Harmonic Wealth' by Charles Arthur Ray. There is a lot to be examined by reading it. Yet I fully understand it. Much like I fully understood when someone said the mind is like a computer . . . only I had a virus churning away 24/7! The virus in my mind, I guess, had made me an anxious, self-conscious person. Now I am training myself to recognise the language used by others to ensure I maintain a healthy mind.

Each day now I see the good side in things to such an extent that possibly people wonder how could someone with short arms feel so good. Maybe they are not looking at the arms at all. Maybe it shows that I feel great. I will certainly keep finding new ways to feel good. Keep doing what works is what some say: well it's true. Why go down paths of self-destruction when a new path of self-creation can be found with the right tools and the right people around you?

I much prefer to be creative than self-destructive. Perhaps the creative side is part of me anyway. Creating something from my thoughts is part of doing it my way. Just that to move a bit further forward the help of others comes in. Then there is a co creation of a product or a better version of oneself. That to me is inspiring!

Doing it my way now has given me more energy than I ever imagined. Having felt that I was driving in a car that had its handbrake on, the energy is now being released. That energy seems to enable me to do so much more with ease.

I suppose having been on this journey for many years—even as a kid—I was trying to do it my way. Other people felt that I should fit in a pigeon hole and perhaps do things the way they do things. In some people's mind a disability still does exactly that: pigeon hole. But birds fly and see what goes on from a higher perspective.

Doing it my way certainly did that: it helped me to see things from different perspective. I had to explore things from so many viewpoints to get to where I am now. Seeing me in different situations, being a happier person in control of where I am going rather than someone who was unhappy and had no control. And if asked to jump I may have said how high. Doing it my way gives me the opportunity to expand my mind, to open up to new ideas and act on them.

'I did it my way' gives me a sense of gratitude. Gratitude that perhaps I never had. I was always thankful for things but perhaps I never looked at the true meaning behind it. Now the gratitude is there even before I do things or ask for help. Feeling grateful for this journey is truly humbling. All the things that have happened good and bad, legal and illegal were for me to give back.

I am lucky to have lived through it. But my thoughts were elsewhere, I had no control over them. Now I do. Those thoughts then could not be controlled without the tools for my mind without practicing, practicing and practicing. At that time, I had no picture of how my life would look in years ahead.

This book is just an insight into my life and a clarification of how I changed my thinking by doing it my way. There is a whole new world to be explored, if you look outside of the box. And looking outside of the box is a progress in itself. This progress and the change of perspective gave me my freedom ☺

Having done it my way

I have learned what works for me. I now keep doing it. TFT, hypnosis, NLP, listening to audio CDs and mp3 . . . If it involves my self-development and opening up my mind to better thinking. I'm up for that! Rays of sunshine now instead of clouds of doom! Light from within at last. My thinking has finally got me to a place of peace: that is to me the best present of my life. I feel now that everything will be all right if I keep doing what I do: be myself!

Victory over myself.

Doing it my way has been a victory, one of my own making. One where I have seen the battles for myself and realised how hard I was fighting. I was struggling just for my own peace. I had to keep going and I did it. Now that the peace has arrived the endorphins flow. A natural high ☺ A high that I hope goes on for the rest of my life. I feel that I learned and opened up my mind to new and exciting opportunities. More opportunities and more possibilities.

Seeing things differently.

Different thinking inspires me! It gives me the chance to think outside of the box. But first of all I had to find a way to get outside of that box: with all that was on my mind the box was keeping me in a dark place. I somehow had to find the light on the outside. Positive thoughts replacing negative thoughts over and over and over again. I literally got to see it in the end.

> *"You have to believe in yourself when no one else does. That's what makes you a winner."*
> **Venus Williams**

The self-belief that I had to get to where I wanted to go has always been there. I do not know why. Perhaps the physical difference was what kept me going: an inner knowing that I could get through the storms and feel calm in the end. A calmness like the eye of a hurricane. Yet I stay in the eye wherever I go.

Never, never, quit.

I felt I could not do that. I perhaps at times wanted to. Yet there was something telling me to keep going. That did not come from other people saying, you can do it or you will get there. Although on occasions they did say that, it came from within. I think that's the same for most people who triumph from their own challenges.

Changing the language I use.

The language that I now use creates the possibility. Possibility leads to so much more. It enables me to go and do things that I never thought of being able to do. My mind had held me back. Now it accelerates me forward.

Mind and body going in one direction.

That to me is awesome. I had felt that, although I wanted to do things and tried, I just kept returning to a place of comfort: a place where nothing was happening. Now I keep going forward and it feels comfortable. Getting used to doing new things from a place of peace. So the new is just another state of mind. A new set of thoughts and feelings and, if I use the tools I have been given, the new is easier to work with. I achieve more and I can do more from this place of peace. The thoughts, feelings and actions going in the same direction. Aligned and being in the flow with life. Just being and doing things because I feel good.

Being vigilant to negativity and open to positivity.

I am now aware of any negative thoughts or influences and I work ways to deflect these from my mind. My heart is open to positive things and that's what keeps me moving forward. Keeping in a positive state of mind. Attracting positive stuff from every situation.

Self-destruction to self-creation

I feel now I am in the process of creating a better life for myself. Having set myself the task of being at peace with myself, I have learned to change. I have learned also to move from a place of destruction to a place of creation, still using my mind but in a way that gives me freedom and choice. I could never have done that a few years ago: I simply did not have the awareness.

Over the years I had felt I had been in a maze.

Going down so many different routes and finding always a dead end. But, as with mazes, there is one path that leads to the centre. The answer come from within, not from the outside. So the final walk through the maze was by releasing all of my past and, in effect, surrendering to it. Allowing myself to just be myself. Removing old negative associations from my mind and creating affirming thoughts. And most of all, starting to follow my heart.

Being more aware of my thoughts.

I had over the years been operating on automatic pilot for destruction. Thoughts disabling me but now are enabling me, I had to see things from a different perspective and re direct my thoughts for good. So doing it my way has given me a choice. A choice to stay put or a choice to move forward :I now always choose to move forward.

Attitude of gratitude.

Gratitude has been something I lacked, over the years. Now I am conscious that this is an everyday blessing in disguise. Being grateful for finding my peace is wonderful. It's liberating and self fulfilling. The gratitude to those that have helped me will always be there. Whilst they opened the door to my mind I eventually walked through.

Now taking command over my life.

By doing it my way I feel I have taken command over my life. It is my life, no one else's. So I am going to allow it to be a life that gives back. To live my life with a purpose.

> *"It is not our purpose to become each other; it is to recognize each other, to learn to see the other and honor him for what he is."*
>
> **Hermann Hesse (1877-1962)**

Chapter 6
Letting go!

"When I let go of what I am, I become what I might be."

Lao Tzu (570-490 BC)

Letting go of the past has been a journey full of ups and downs. I have been moving forward, releasing the resistance of my old feelings as I go along, allowing a healthier life, full of love, wealth and happiness.

I was comfortable with keeping safe, avoiding certain things in life. Now, by letting go, I start to believe more in myself and do better things. I want to help others, yet, to do so, I have to help myself. And this is what I do now. But there have been many roadblocks in the way, most of them at an unconscious level. But as the iceberg melts, the subconscious thoughts come to the surface and then disappear. That is happening now, by creating new beliefs so that I can move forward. These new beliefs are the stepping stones to my future.

One of the hardest things in my life, I guess, was to accept myself. I found this difficult. I never met anyone similar to me until I was 28, so I never felt part of the norm. I tried hard to succeed, to be like everyone else. But for some reason I just wanted to be myself. Although my arms are different to others they are a part of me, part of the whole. By letting go of the fact that my arms are different, even if unique to me, I began incorporating this to be a whole human being.

I can look back now and feel I needed to go through what I have to get to where I am now. The roadblocks that have been there were painful. Anxiety, depression and significant challenges with alcohol have played an important part. I find hard to believe I went through all of that. I am a nice person: I did not want what happened. What a waste if the music within me just dies and I give nothing back!

My head was muddled for approximately 30 years. I did not know why I had certain feelings: I kept a hold of the fact that these thoughts were a product of not feeling comfortable. I felt a sense of fear. That fear led me to avoid many social situations. I was fearful of being looked at. Fearful of people touching my hands. Fearful of people asking questions about my hands and the way they are.

I needed to turn it around. But how? How could I find a way past all of that? The techniques shown to me have worked. They gave me a start. A stepping stone and look how far I seem to be going. New stepping stones seem to be falling in the right place. The fear seems to be going away. What I do feel now is a sense of loving myself for who I am. The arms are part of me, the essence of me and are the success of me.

I want to let go of the old me. I can let go of the old me. The old me has gone. These are the thoughts that enable me to move forward. Sometimes we see change as being extremely difficult: I am no different. But it does get easier. And, in the end, for some reason the change seems effortless.

I am still wondering if I have to find out why: there seems to be the odd 'eureka' moment as new inspired thoughts enter my mind. I try to act on these thoughts to avoid falling back into the old me. It seems that letting go of the old me is giving me a new lease of life. A life of feeling much happier, more confident and knowing that the changes are for the best.

The old thoughts of how I looked disabled me: now, with these new thoughts and clarity of mind, the thoughts about my arms are enabling me. Letting go, to grow springs to mind. Not my arms if any of you are thinking that way! ☺

The books, audios, cds and coaching have helped me in so many ways that—the old thoughts that were buried deep in my mind—are now at the surface to be let go of. Much like an iceberg melting. There is now no judgment of those who were part of my life of turmoil. The anger within has gone to reveal a loving, happier person who is free. Sometimes too carefree, but I love it!☺

May be the timing of what has happened was meant to be. Somehow things seem to be harder to get done, if you push them. By letting go of past thoughts and being much more present with what is happening in my life now, I see that more gets done. I wish I had known that years ago. Feeling frustrated and resentful will not help: that only adds to the problem. To not have the bad thoughts of my arms is now a reality of mine. Letting go lead to peace and freedom, clarity of mind: a sense of being at one at last.

I have dealt with all of this with a journey of my own making: I find it very interesting. I chose one way or another to follow certain paths. Some in not such a great state of mind, others with clarity and direction. It also may have been frustrating for family and friends to see that letting go has been something I have always wanted. To have a feeling of being at one with who I am gives rise to being able to talk about my arms freely.

Maybe age and maturity has something to do with it. Some at work may chuckle at the thought of maturity. I wrote a poem a few years ago describing my feelings and that will to let go:

> *'Letting go of me is what I want A life of denial is no good to me*
> *A year of purpose zest and life no more worrying, no more strife*
> *A railway track I see in front of me two lives converging, just like*
> *me one of denial, one of acceptance no more anger no more fear*
> *tears of joy I see in front of me, a part of me has now become free*
> *Life is full of surprises, I have seen: look forward and follow your*
> *dreams.'* ☺

This was much about me putting some thoughts on paper. The railway track is simply a metaphor: when seen over a distance, the lines seem to converge into ONE. Denial and acceptance were coming together. The acceptance is what I wanted but I had to let go of the denial: it was of no real use to me. Could I lead a fulfilling life in denial of my arms? Somehow I think differently about the whole thing. The acceptance seems to be much easier now. I like myself as I am. The part that looks different is . . . just different.

For some, the above may be a bit confusing. The railway track bit was one of coming together and joining the parts of me that perhaps had been separated over the years. Never thought of the acceptance until now: the anger was always a part of me that kept coming out in many different ways. When the two tracks come together, I can change and move on to a different track (acceptance) and move away towards a happier life by being at one with myself.

'Holding on to anger, resentment and hurt only gives you tense muscles, a head ache and a sore jaw from clenching your teeth. Forgiveness gives you back the laughter and lightness in your life.

Joan Lunden

This quote seemed to be so true for so many years. People could see the tension in me and, no doubt, wanted the best for me. Now looking at what I see in others I only want the best for them. I remember friends saying they could see the worry lines on my face: a bit different now. The smile has returned. ☺ There seems to be a sense of allowing things to occur, instead of using fear and anxiety to stop things from happening.

Letting go of a part of me now seems more therapeutic than I realise. I now focus on my energy going into the good things. Having found a part of me that I now love, my energy levels have gone up. I can use this energy to focus on things that I now want in my life. The idea of this book was in my mind already 10 years ago but I did not have the energy to write it. The letting go of low level thinking has given rise to something quite miraculous.

There is now a willingness to see things differently, with an open mind. Something that gives myself a chance to help others. Something that I would now love to do. I can now give back my knowledge without the emotions that went with it. Family and friends can see a new improved version of me: the version that loves life without holding himself back with self-destructive thoughts. At the moment, there is a wonderful feeling that, at this stage of my life, I am at my best, rather than better than anyone else.

Letting go of my old thoughts, got me to feel free. Feeling free much like an eagle soaring over the mountains, looking things just as they are. I feel I can walk and talk about me with a sense of purpose, with a sense of direction that is new but exciting and adventurous. Maybe that same sense of adventure has returned from when I was a very young child when I had been posted to different countries. It was an adventure for a child. I wonder how adventurous it is for forces children today . . .

The journey to let go has taken many years and some of the readers may ask to themselves if I really changed and how. Well there are so many tools I am using to help me: self-improvement is one of the most fascinating. My mind is simply changing with the new thoughts I have: better and more empowering beliefs that give me a sense of purpose.

Thoughts of loving myself and the situations I put myself in, rather than fearing things. I kept asking for help, I persevered, never quitting. Sometimes taking a breather, yes, but never quitting. It is paying off now and I feel at peace and free with it all. I was always ASKING.

> *'You are important enough to ask and you are blessed enough to receive back'.*
>
> **Wayne Dyer**
> **(Self-development author and speaker).**

I realise I did ask many times: the unconscious thoughts were the ones that needed to be let go of but I was not asking for the right tools to help me do that. I was always fighting fires and unable to prevent them: now I can prevent the fires with the awareness of the thoughts that I have.

The process of letting go of these old thinking patterns is another new journey that I am on. I now feel happier within and know that, having a sense of control over the thoughts, is my success. Hence the title being 'Success in my hands' : a journey to be happy with 'my arms' by loving them.

> *'Success is not the key to happiness. Happiness is the key to success. If you love what you are doing, you will be successful'*
>
> **Albert Schweitzer**

Letting go enables me to live a life in a purposeful direction and doing things better by being in a better state of mind. I am starting to see happiness all around me. I choose happier thoughts about me.

Even my mother once said: 'You are now comfortable in your own skin'. This journey is great: I feel empowered and free from particular thoughts.

I am also proud to have not just done this for myself, although that is a huge part of it.: I have done this also for my parents and sister. Hence the book is dedicated to them: I think that every parent wants what is best for their children.

Letting go has also much to do with trusting that all will be ok. I now believe that, what will happen over the years to come, will be ok. There's now a trust in what I want to achieve in my life. If I was brought into this world to help others by having to go through what I have, then it has been worth it if I give it back a different way. I want to learn as much as I can about myself so that I can say to others that there is always a way around things, when the thinking is changed.

For some reason as I write this, forgiveness comes to mind. Over the years, I have felt that other people have had an impact on how I see my arms. It is important to realise that I may have unknowingly chosen to have those thoughts. By forgiving those, I release my resentment and anger toward such people. The peace within has arrived.

Letting go of the anger has allowed me to find a peace of mind. There appears to have been a shift in my thinking that, few years ago, I could never have imagined Also I feel I am beginning to connect better with people. Giving other people their time to talk to me was sometimes something I didn't do. When you connect with other people there is a better rapport and things seem to happen with relative ease. The letting go of how I felt about myself is getting so much easier now.

This seems to happen in every area of my life. Work and recreation are better, easier and I feel I can give value back simply by being a better person. In some way, by letting go, the old energy that was draining other people has gone.

Although it is understandable for me to talk about my old feelings of myself, I know that they drain energy out of myself and, no doubt, of other people. Understandable that, if the energy is being withdrawn, people may not always have time for you. So by finding and using the right tools for me I have realised that I have more energy. I can now look at my arms from a different perspective and—in some cases—even joke about them.

Simple things now make me laugh: getting things out of the fridge and, on the odd occasion, bumping my head on the top of the fridge as I can't reach far enough to get some things out☺

The psychological stress of dealing with the look of my arms on a day to day basis is now non existent. I am able to keep the old thoughts at bay with tools I have had the luxury of obtaining. Thought field therapy is the tool that I use each day. As I have spent much of my life in a frame of mind that was self-defeating I vow now to keep my mind in a healthy state.

The trauma of days gone by is becoming less and less : I am calmer now than I have been for many years. I have also noticed that people are much more at ease with me: they help me to get things done. Often our thoughts are reflected back by our experiences: thinking happier thoughts seems to get happier experiences.

I was always looking and seeking help: friends and family can vouch for this. I guess they didn't know what to do other than listen to what my concerns were. I somehow had to correct a way of thinking. It seemed so out of balance.

> *'When you correct your mind, all things fall in to place'.*
> **Lao Ztu (604-531 B.C.)**

Since letting go of my old thinking, I am beginning to create a life of my own making. I am learning to think about 'what if I did this'. Much like saying I am going to be in a 'what if up club' ☺, where the 'what ifs' are all positive gains in my life.

As I write this book, I am thinking about what if this book could help other people who want to change their thoughts about themselves.

My emotions linked in with my arms seemed to hold me back. The frustration of not knowing how to deal with things seemed to be evident in many areas of my life: I did not know how to balance my emotions.

"When you develop your ability to balance your emotions, unexpected problems won't knock you off balance as easily, and you'll return more quickly to a positive outlook."

Peggy McColl New York Times Best Selling Author

I think that children are probably the most inquisitive: they are direct with their questioning because they see something different. They ask: 'Why are your arms like that? I respond: 'I was born like it' and smile ☺ Parents sometimes apologise for their children. They needn't! Do I apologise for having short arms? It's just a question and letting go enables me to deal with it from a better frame of mind.

What intrigues me the most is the length of time that it has taken to get to where I am! 30 years of self-defeating thinking has given me a story. Would I look back and say to myself what would have I done differently. Hind sight is always a great thing. But, in some strange way, what didn't work for me . . . was working for me. Whilst I was in a self-defeating pattern of thought, the paradox is that now things are now working for me, since having found the tools to let go of these thought patterns.

Since using these tools I have found happiness in my life. 'Success in my hands' is the paradox: I feel joyful in so many things.

"The only true measure of success is the amount of joy we are feeling."

Abraham-Hicks

It seems that I now have the opportunity to lead a new life. A joyful one as I feel good with all is happening. I hope it lasts: I trust that it will last. I expect that, by letting go, more successful things will happen. If I look back, I now see that much of the journey was stepping stones to where I am now.

Some may say that, having short arms, problems will possibly arise. Well, I see them as obstacles and stepping stones to moving forward. I can place each stone in front of the other in whatever direction I wish to take while removing barriers from my vocabulary and replacing them with stepping stones.

The barriers simply do not exist anymore. It amazes me that, by not thinking about my arms as a means to hold me back, I am able to substitute that thought with another which guides me to where I want to go. So, by having positive thoughts about me, I can go on and do positive things. By doing so, also my energy levels increase.

I now get to decide which stepping stones I have to put in front of me: that's why I want to assist others with forming their own stepping stones to where they want to get to, enabling them to think new thoughts of happiness.

Letting go of what people have said to me about my arms, creates a space in my mind to fill with something else. Emptying my mind of negativity and of 30 years of unconstructive thinking, I would allow myself to have the positive thoughts. Avoiding a void, feeling what next, what if?

The strangest thing is that now I AM comfortable in my own skin. The thoughts were something I held on to keep me from moving forward. I kept giving myself a story of why I could not have what I wanted. Work, relationships, money and even health, in some cases. The whole of my life was impacted by a set of stories I kept telling myself.

> *"The only thing holding you back is the story you keep telling yourself as to why you can't have it"*
> **Tony Robbins**

Looking back, maybe from school age, I realise I could have given myself a different story. A story where I would have been ok with the arms that I have, not caring about other people's thoughts about them. I want my thoughts to be positive and complimentary as if to say I deserve things just like everyone else.

> *"Scars remind us where we've been—they don't have to dictate where we are going."*
> **Joe Mantegna**
> **Actor**

The scars from years gone by have healed. It may even be that, by writing this, it is therapy in itself. Turning things around so those scars, whilst not visible on the surface, have little or no impact on my life as I go forward. Progress has been, in some way, seeing the same things differently. There is a sense that, by letting go, one develops a more improved mental toughness.

There is an inner knowing that everything will be ok. Trusting the process that I am going through to achieve all that I want in life. It feels like I am in a race, but the only competitor is me. Me against myself, or, if you like, the old person prior the techniques I have been taught, against the newer version. It can also be said that, for example, when you let go of something—e.g. drinking, smoking etc.—you become something different. Something new. You may like it. I love the new me.

I like to use the word NOW because, if you turn it around, it spells WON. By living in the NOW, with no thoughts of my past, I have WON. I am at peace. Seeing things just as they are. Living on purpose.

The new journey starts now, deciding on what I want to do with the rest of my life. With all the experiences of my past, to now do good with those experiences and enable others to have an opportunity to let go of what they made need to.

My focus for what I want to achieve is there: letting go has enabled me to do so.

> *"To have faith in oneself and become something of worth and value is the best and safest course."*
> **Michelangelo (1475-1564)**

I somehow knew I would get there, finding peace with myself and having faith in doing so: I just didn't know how. Holding onto old thoughts, held my self-worth back, I didn't value myself. Now with new thoughts of value and self-worth I am finally on a safe course. The new thoughts form a springboard from which I can leap on to new things. To a new life.

Changing my thinking, visualising a new life, finding new ways to perform better are all things I want to do. For some reason, changing my inner thoughts seems to have changed my outer experiences.

People seem different to me now, they are at ease with me just as I am at ease with myself. How could this be? My thoughts about myself have changed. I feel happier, richer and I know all that is on the way is for the best. My past experiences form a foundation for me. But that foundation, in one sense, was weak and full of cracks: it needed reinforcing. Now I can stand on it knowing that it is strong and stable.

There is a power in letting things go: I no longer hold on to something that keeps me weighed down. I allow things just to happen, each person that I meet offers something new. Instead of declining things based on what I felt of myself, I try to allow them based on the fact that all will be ok. People like to give when they can, I guess we all do. By giving, it feels like the focus is no longer on me but on someone else. My thoughts about myself diminish and I can help others with whatever they need to do.

The frustration, fear and anxiety related to my arms have gone. Without using TFT each day and many other tools to help me with developing a positive mindset, I would be in a different place, no doubt. I also am aware of my own self talk. I carefully select words that are positive. The more positive thoughts I have, the less negative thoughts impact my life.

The balance in my thinking is on track with where I want to go in my life. I consciously make decisions each day to keep in a positive mental attitude. Choosing to let go of the old and choosing to create new positive thoughts.

There is now a passion to keep thinking good thoughts: I am astounded by the process that I am going through. It's like I am rewiring the circuitry in my brain. Much of my old thinking was short circuiting and creating problems. The thoughts were low energy thoughts, giving me things like depression, anxiety and panic attacks. High energy thoughts now give me a sense of being in a state of happiness, feeling healthy and creating positive opportunities.

'When I let go of what I am, I become what I might be.'
Lao Tzu (c.604-531 B.C.)

Now I have found a means and a purpose to let go of my past. I have found a sense of gratitude in everything that is coming my way. Gratitude towards those who are now part of my new life. Gratitude to those who support me to do good with the physical difference that I have. Most of all, gratitude to being given this wonderful opportunity to change my thinking. I could have thought in a victim mindset for the rest of my life but now I feel empowered and I believe I can achieve all that I want to achieve. Asking for help, believing that the help will be right for me and receiving the help that I asked for. Trusting that all will turn out ok.

'What you get by reaching your destination is not nearly as important as what you will become by reaching your destination."

Zig Ziglar

The journey I have taken to let go of my past has been a long one. 30 years of holding on to old thinking patterns is effectively three quarters of my lifetime. No one can say that I didn't try to change: I just didn't know how. I have learnt so much over the last few years, realising that past thoughts of negativity must be kept away to enable me to live a meaningful life.

By reaching this destination, I can perhaps offer some kind of hope to others. Their journey to their destination may not need to take as long as mine. I hope that by letting go I can make a difference in people's lives, much as they have made a difference in mine.

I am in the process of keeping my old thoughts at bay. It is like I am reprogramming my brain for success. Having a success mindset with all that I want to do. I cannot control some of the events that happen around me but I make sure the events can be used to create a path to a new destination. It seems that letting go has much more of an impact on my life than I realised.

Things around me are improving. The plans that I make I know will succeed. Adjustments may be necessary, much like an aircraft on a flight path to somewhere new: always making adjustments. I am sure that, over the years, I had a destination in mind. There was a plan to get to a sense of peace: I knew I would get there. But the plan needed other people to assist me and, most of all, I had to do it my way!

By letting go of these old thoughts, I am just me. Taking the negative out of my mind. Labeling myself with me. This is who I am. A happy, kind and thoughtful person, wanting to do good with the experiences that I have had. Things then change. The thoughts I have now become my reality. Good thoughts about myself gives me a fulfilling reality.

The feeling of just being happy with the body I have is amazing. All those years where I couldn't do stuff are in the past. My thoughts about me held me back: the thoughts of me now propel me forward.

So, in essence, what did I have to do to enable me to let go?

Being willing to do something.

Where there is a will there is a way. How true. Put in the work and the results will be revealed. Letting go is much about trusting in myself. Believing that, having gone on a path that didn't work—although paradoxically it did—I kept holding on to my thoughts of the past. They kept me stuck in every area of my life: health, wealth, relationships and much more. With letting go of those thoughts as if they were a ship sailing off to an island, I become detached from them and they disappear. I had to let go and allow the wind of change to blow in another direction. A new ship now arrives bringing with it a cargo of riches to spice things up a bit. Letting go has created room for me to add zing to my life and create whatever I want.

Changing the fuel for the fire.

Whilst over much of my lifetime I had been adding the wrong fuel to keep going, I now realised I was constantly supplying the fire and keeping it burning by repeating the same thoughts of negativity. Adding to it with a mixture of alcohol and then hiding away. Now things are very much different: the fuel is knowledge. Knowledge that, by changing my thoughts of myself and letting go, I become a different human being. One who is happier and at peace ☺. The letting go seems to have allowed a new fuel for this fire. A spirit! Inspired to change myself for all the right reasons. To love and cherish who I am. ☺

Always looking for solutions.

I have now found solutions that keep on working. TFT, hypnosis, NLP, visualisation and so on. They are all wonderful ways of getting me to where I want to go from the point I am now. Constantly looking forward. My T-shirt from the past was a bit worn out and tattered: I now have a new one. A Totally Unique T-shirt that keeps me motivated to do more and inspires me to be the best I can be with the body I have. I feel complete and whole.

Being Authentic to who I really am

I now feel that letting go brings in something new. A new life for me now although I feel the past has taught me a valuable lesson. One so profound that I can now give back what I have learned in such a short space of time. The past has taught me to love and be kind, be generous and be true to myself. Be authentic and allow the good to come into my life instead of pushing it away. Life is like a mirror: it is a reflection of oneself. Feel happy and others with feel happy around you. Be at peace and others will feel the same.

Changing track to a course for greater things.

Making my own track. letting go of the track I was on. The poem that I wrote near the beginning of this chapter reveals I was on a separate track, mainly one of anger. Yet by letting go of the old and accepting who I am, whole and perfect, I allow acceptance to flood into my life. The two tracks, seen as they approach the horizon, become one. They come together to take me on a new journey through life. A happier and loving one. ☺

Realising that holding on kept me in the same place.

Letting go takes me to lots of new and exciting places. Places where I feel free and at peace, places that offer exactly the same. Letting go gave me the freedom that I deserved: no more comments of how I look, no more negative thoughts of myself. Those old thoughts from my childhood are gone. I can now look back with the wisdom of those experiences and view life from a higher perspective.

Realising calmness comes after letting go.

A thought that now is in my reality at last. The old days of feeling stressed and unhappy within are gone. A calm and solid self-assurance is here to stay as I develop a foundation for being a certain way. Being whole and perfect just as I am. Allowing thoughts to flow through my everyday experiences and feeling at ease with the course of life, instead of trying to fight it.

Letting go gives me more energy.

From all of the hard work I have put in to my own self-development, I have gained much more energy to do so much more. I can use that energy to give back to others who may be on a similar path to mine. I have sometimes questioned this path. Why I am on it and why I have taken so long to find the end of it? I admit it has taken near enough 30 years to find this peace. But the letting go of the old allows the new to grow. New seeds are being planted each day to blossom into a different human being. A human being who is better than he used to be. One who trusts and one who loves. Now a clearer reflection of himself.

Trusting that all will be ok.

I got to a stage where I began to trust this process of change. The change has come about in a relatively short space of time yet, somehow, I believe and trust in the process. I believe I have won my battles over myself. No more fighting and resisting change. Now I allow to change for the better not only for me but for everyone else I meet.

Knowing that life can be full of adventure and excitement.

This is what happens when I have let go of my past. The new adventure has started and I am excited by it. By letting go there is a swagger about me:

an inner knowing that now everything will be ok, no matter what. I have sailed through peaks and stormy waters and through what would seem a hurricane. But, as with hurricanes, there is the eye where is calm and the sun shines. I feel that I am in the eye but I finally know how to move with it and flow with it, rather than thinking of what will happen when the eye passes over me. I am learning the calmness, the ability to be still in my mind more often. The clearness derived from letting go of my past and allowing happier circumstances to come into my life. The adventure of seeing life how it actually is rather, than fighting to get to be a part of it.

Letting go gives me inspiration.

That human spirit that we all have is now being realized, giving me the reason to learn more and the inspiration that I needed. That inspiration creates a better life for me by forming and attracting positive thoughts. Thoughts that lifted me to a better place: a place where I can now give back instead of always taking

Tired of the patterns: something had to change.

My outer world or my inner: the inner worked! By realising that the past thoughts created a pattern of having and loosing things, I had to find the calmness in my life. This calmness—or peace—allows things to come into my life much quicker. Happy circumstances appear so much faster. Now I am STILL learning but the stillness seems to bring a sense of joy and abundance whereas, previously, chaos brought disordered things in my life. The U turn seems to create more and the happier I feel the more things seem to happen. It is like a sense of returning home.

Enjoyment at last

I feel I can enjoy life the way it is meant to be, living in harmony with everything around me. The harmony with life, I guess, was something I felt would happen in the end. After all, if I had been disconnected with who I truly am then the opposite would occur if I connected with who I am. Taking a U turn again to get a better result.

> *Success is not the key to happiness. Happiness is the key to success. If you love what you are doing, you will be successful.*
>
> **Albert Schweitzer**

As this journey continues, I become happier and happier. It does feel weird, sometimes, knowing that this feeling is here to stay. Finding my own peace within has brought along with it the happiness that I desired in the first place. I had spent years convincing others that I was ok although they knew inside that I wasn't. Now it is so much different. A transformation from a human being that, in effect, was almost on his knees hoping for someone else to change the circumstances to someone who creates his circumstances, through much better thinking and a focus on achieving what his heart desires. Follow your heart: so true!

Letting go gave me a new direction

Now I am a free thinker instead of someone who absorbs other people's thoughts. With the freedom to think for myself and to create what I want in my life, the direction I look is . . . forward. Letting go gave me the ability to think now and ahead, expanding my mind instead of killing it with negative thinking. That's what depression and anxiety were doing to me. I got to put a stop to it and without drugs: I made the choice!

The Power of thoughts

Well after what I know now, I will never think the same again! No! Why? Because I have empowered myself. The enablement has come from thinking empowering thoughts. Thoughts that enable. Thoughts that come from within. Heartfelt thoughts. Thoughts that are passionate with a view that I want to see others happy. It is achievable even when you are on your knees. From there, the only way is up! ☺

Peace of mind has given me clarity

The peace of mind has given me clarity and the feeling of being carefree. Compassionate yes, but with a sense I can be more caring with letting go of the attachment I had with myself. Just being and going with the flow.

The detachment works wonders. Having been born on an island now I see it much more clearly: if my thoughts were to be considered the mainland then, by separating from my thoughts, I am less attached. The detachment creates a gap which allows something to come in between. This creates space. Space for a solution or for a view from a different perspective.

Letting go leads to 'What if I did'!

Everything that comes my way now I think 'what if I did do this'? Who knows I will be able to see the results as I do. Holding on led me to not doing something: I had a blame mentality and that was not going to work for me. The 'what if' leads to imagination. Imagine doing something that, with a sense of great feeling, I achieve. This book is leading me to be inspired to do other things. I kind of knew it would. But for the first time in my life, I have created something very special to me to be seen by others. My heart is now open to allow whatever comes my way. Letting go has done that for me.

Paradoxes

Well 30 years of what was not working for me (my thinking) has lead me to a sense of what was working for me. I can see the transformation myself. I am still astounded. Who was that person a few years ago? How could he change? I am in awe of those who have helped me. They are the ones behind the scenes that have made all their work worthwhile. They have helped turn the key to unlock me. They found the right combination to unlock the door and let go of the old and allow all of the new. I say the new because that's how it feels. But I now realise it was there all along. I just needed to connect with it.

Stepping stones: I now create them.

Stepping onto one in front of the other. Going in the direction that I want. I am the driver of this car without the brakes on. This car seems to weave in and out through the traffic at speed, with ease. A car that is moving into fifth gear where the mind is relatively slow but is going somewhere fast.

Letting go has opened up my heart.

To allow, to forgive and to live my life how it is meant to be. To follow my dreams and see where they take me. Life is an adventure when it is taken less seriously. Look at nature. Dolphins play and leap in the sea: I have lived on an island where this happened each day. To see nature as it is meant to be. Just as it is! No ifs or buts. It is! I now look at my life and, by being me, I am the maker of my own path.

At EASE. Ironically a military term.

At ease and standing easy! I feel that now. I find I am standing tall and at ease with all that is going on around me. The ease seems now to be natural. Natural in the fact that much of my life was meant to be easy, thoughts of making it difficult got in the way. Thoughts from childhood about how I should be rather than how I am. Still better late than never. Letting go has given me the opportunity to see it now.

'Progress, seeing the same things differently'—Kevin Laye.

Well I see things differently now. What an awesome change. Transformed from a someone who found resistance to much of his life to one of allowing to all to come his way. The whole turnaround is still astounding and I am sure more astounding things are to follow now that I am on a new path. A path that I am creating, instead of one where I followed.

Forgiveness

Forgiveness seems to take the sting out of what has happened over the years: it provides a sense of ease. Knowing that others said what they said as they knew no different: I didn't at the time either. I also have forgiven myself for going on certain paths that led to self-defeating attitudes and creating a path of destruction. Letting go of all of that is a key to a lock that allows something special into my life.

Gratitude

Letting go has given me an attitude of gratitude. I feel grateful for knowing this path that I have gone on was meant to be. Meant to be so that, at some point, I would wake up and see life for what it really is. It is supposed to be loving, joyful and full of opportunities to create whatever your heart desires. My heart's desire to find that sense of peace and love for who I am rather than for how I look.

Daring to dream.

Well letting go has given me a willingness to make my dreams come true. Imagination provides a starting point to create something new. Even my own peace has been created through imagining that I would get to this point in my life. It certainly was something that I was looking to achieve even at the age of 13/14. Other cogs were moving in my mind to get me to see things differently in the end. I just didn't know it, then.

Switching things 180 degrees

Dislike to like, fearing to loving. Through that along comes a feeling. A feeling of joy that I have done it at last. Reversing thoughts and connecting with them. One thought that feels good, connects with another that feels good and so on. Letting go the old and allow the new. Trusting in the process 100 per cent.

Perfecting my thoughts: practice practice practice!

Creating a new programme for my mind. The old programme , as it were, was tuned in for everything that was self-destructive. By perfecting my thoughts, thinking better, practicing each and every day, I become a better person each and every day. I change. Simply by changing my thoughts my life changes from the inside: the outside seems to be different to what I have been used to.

The rights steps for me.

> *'A journey of a thousand miles must begin with a single step'*
>
> **Lao Tzu**

In one respect, that step started by going to Harley Street. I was shown a door, I walked through it. The timing in my life was perfect, in every way. I did not force myself to go: I allowed myself to go. There is a difference. Letting go is part of a process of allowing to enable. It has enabled me to move further, faster and higher and, in one way, with relative ease. As if it is meant to be this way: I now know I just follow it.

Shifting from one way of thinking to another

It seems a shift has occurred with my thinking, almost overnight. Yet I know the shift has taken a few years but it is not that much to remove old poor conditioning and allowing in improved thoughts which give me a choice in what I want to be and where I want to go. The letting go has giving me that choice. To be someone and to go somewhere: each of those being a choice of mine by connecting with an inner part of me rather than reacting to outer circumstances.

From the heart.

The heart desires but my mind acquires. The heart allows for my feelings to be known and now my mind seems to find a way of finding what my heart desires. It already has with the peace of mind. I truly wanted peace with all my heart. I feel it and it feels real to me. Authentic. ☺

Inside out approach

I tried the outside approach: it didn't work. I kept doing what other people suggested. See a doctor, go on medication, counselling, talk and talk. Somehow that was not me. I felt there was something wrong with me. I was just disconnected with who I really am. A spirited human being who loves life and loves others when in tune with it.

My compass setting.

Now my compass setting is one for true North, giving me the opportunity to be myself and fixing a new direction in line with it. I feel now that my journey up to now has been on a compass setting but one that has kept moving around. I got lost simply by not using it properly. A compass is a tool to get me to where I want to be. But to dismiss its value and its purpose simply can lead to a life that ends with its music still in me. With an authentic compass setting, the music within me will be shown along the way. I hope letting go gives me the opportunity to play in a playground that life is meant to be. It is up to me.

There is a smile coming from within.

People seem to be smiling back. So I must be doing something right. I seem to now be completely trusting as I let go. Enough is enough and with the tools I have to hand, I can now appreciate this new process.

Each day I ensure I keep positive. Written statements are nearby to help me to keep going. Books are always nearby for me to read: I have my own personal library. I'm inquisitive about how this change has happened. I didn't deliberately choose years ago to hold on and wait until I was 40, to release my past and go on to do better things.

Letting go is allowing things to slot into place. I have better relationships with people, which is something that I always wanted. But how could I have better relationships with people if I didn't have a better relationship with myself? If I feel good about myself, the chances are I would feel better about other people. I would be able to give more of myself to other people and they would be able to give back.

The process has also enabled me to think clearer.

The fog has lifted. A fog that has clouded my mind for nearly 30 years. This clearing offers me the opportunity to see things on distant horizons. To view things from each area of my life, health, wealth, happiness, relationships. Each of these has been affected over the years because I was stuck in a mindset that was self-defeating. How could any of these work out the way I wanted to when part of me didn't let go of the thoughts of my arms?

> *"Be careful what you water your dreams with. Water them with worry and fear and you will produce weeds that choke the life from your dream. Water them with optimism and solutions and you will cultivate success. Always be on the lookout for ways to turn a problem into an opportunity for success. Always be on the lookout for ways to nurture your dream."*
>
> **Lao Tzu**

Being better than I used to be

Perhaps I was always trying to perfect me. I couldn't change my outer appearance but I could change the way I thought about it! I think now with my arms as they are: just me. I must admit to myself: I cope remarkably well. The body is an amazing thing. The mind is even better. To perfect a way of thinking that overcomes the way we think of ourselves is, to me, the cool bit. What is even cooler is that I can now do this for the rest of my life. Letting go and living as I was meant to live, free from the psychological turmoil that I had created over the years.

> *"Learn to enjoy every minute of your life. Be happy now. Don't wait for something outside of yourself to make you happy in the future. Think how really precious is the time you have to spend, whether it's at work or with your family. Every minute should be enjoyed and savoured."*
>
> **Earl Nightingale**
> **1921-1989, Radio Announcer, Author and Speaker**

Shifting the focus

Helping others shifts the focus away from me. Whilst I am aware of my own physical difference, I realise I can do good with it. Instead of the old me hiding and retreating to avoid the good things in life we all deserve-health, wealth and happiness—I feel I am now on a path to attract all of this.

By letting go of thoughts of what others expected from me, I can start to attract the 'what if I can' being positive in everything I do.

> *"Release Others' Expectations. If you focus on what others expect of you, you' ll continue to act on and attract more of what they desire for you. But when you can shift your inner thoughts to what you intend to create and attract into your life, you will no longer have to give mental energy to what others want for you . . . ."—*
>
> **Dr. Wayne Dyer**

Removing the 'dis' out of disability

Replacing it with capability, adaptability and I am sure many more words to focus on, away from limitations based on how we think. There are no limits when you start using the tools for the mind. There are many people out there that helped me with letting go of my limiting thoughts with the right tools. I feel there are no limits to achieve what I set out to do.

Each day that I have, I value it as something special. Whilst I cannot change my past, nor would I wish to, I can now use the knowledge that I have acquired to provide a compelling future. That future starts with this book.

Being capable engages me into finding the right tools, thoughts and people to achieve the required task. Short arms or no short arms my mind adapts to finding the solution to accomplish the outcome.

I seem now to tune into feeling happy. Letting go of the old thoughts as if I was saying goodbye to an old friend. A friend that I kept purely because I did not know or want to say goodbye to. I wake up each day with new thoughts in my mind. One of a sense of calm and tranquillity. These are the thoughts I carry with me on a day to day basis. The chaos I had in my mind is now over. That's the way I intend it to be.

By being calm, people around me are calm. That is something a few years ago people never felt. Perhaps they saw something unfamiliar that made them feel uncomfortable. I was uncomfortable with myself then: how could people help me if they felt uncomfortable around me?

By holding on to the old thoughts, I could not allow space in my mind for anything else. That space, seemingly was health, wealth, happiness and so much more. I simply did not give myself the chance to have all of this. I tried but I felt comfortable with the old. Now, with the new, I can give myself a better chance to make things work.

Letting go to give way to inspiration.

Inspiration has come from somewhere within. Maybe I didn't want to leave this planet without doing something. If I left without adding to the world what a waste of my own life that would be. To not give back would have been selfish and self-centred. To give is a way of loving oneself and loving others irrespective of a person's difference. Having found the inspiration I am determined to dedicate time to help others. Time is so valuable and, whilst much of my life was consumed with thoughts of myself, now is the time to value all that life has to offer.

> *"Life is too short to waste. Dreams are fulfilled only through action, not through endless planning to take action."*
>
> **David J. Schwartz**
> **Trainer and Author**

This process of letting go has enabled me to focus.

To detach myself from the thoughts surrounding my arms and to start living the life I am meant to have. Life should be easy, I have just got in the way. I prevented many things from coming into my life simply by not focus away from my arms.

I took action to find the right tools for me to enable me to change the thinking. But now there is a source of inspiration. If I can change the way

I think about me, then by writing this book, those that want to change may find the right tools for them.

The action I now take is one of filling my mind with as much positive stuff as I can find. Having learned from the fact that I attracted so much negative stuff over the years, I have now found the way to attract the positive stuff. I keep going, I keep giving myself positive things to think about. I think of how I would like to feel. More good feelings come along. A laugh, a smile: sometimes is all that it takes. ☺

Taking 100% responsibility for myself

Means that all of my actions are in line with me thinking in the right way. Letting go has enabled me to think of my health, going to the gym to keep in shape. Doing a mental work out to keep my mind in shape. That work out consists of some meditation, visualization, affirmations and TFT, which I use everyday.

The other and most important choice of all is responsibility. Over the years, I looked at my arms as something that gave me permission to not care about things. That resulted in abusing alcohol, creating financial problems, work going the wrong way: I was not taking full responsibility for all of this. I was on a course of self-destruction.

The new direction brings in with it all the help that I ask for.

Part of that is believing in myself. Having a sense of self-worth, knowing that I deserve to have all the good things life has to offer. The compass is now set to a true North. This gives me a sense of setting things that I want in my life. A life where I can simply be myself: a spirited person who enjoys feeling good. After all those years of being low in mood, my life is directed so that I can feel good as often as I can.

This time I am allowing all those good feelings to come into my life. It is like I have found me: I have finally found what I was looking for. The peace ☺

> *"It's not what's happening to you now or what has happened in your past that determines who you become. Rather, it's your decisions about what to focus on, what things mean to you, and what you're going to do about them that will determine your ultimate destiny."*
> **Anthony Robbins**

Letting go of my focus upon my arms and feeling negative at an unconscious level has now lead to a new focus. To focus on creating new possibilities for myself. To focus on creating new thoughts to live a better life. To focus on changing the language I use, from disabling to enabling and beyond.

> *'If you focus on results, you will never change. If you focus on change, you will get results.'*
> **Jack Dixon**

Letting go resulted in one big change. I became ME ☺

Chapter 7
Looking Forward

"Man often becomes what he believes himself to be. If I keep on saying to myself that I cannot do a certain thing, it is possible that I may end by really becoming incapable of doing it. On the contrary, if I have the belief that I can do it, I shall surely acquire the capacity to do it even if I may not have it at the beginning."

Mahatma Gandhi (1869-1948)

Now what a good feeling it is to look forward! I realise the past is the past and that cannot change. I NOW focus on being happy as I am but with a vision for what will come my way. Much like an architect designs a house: I look forward to projecting how I would like my life to be. I have seen how it works thinking negatively: what about the possibilities when I think positively? ☺

What I think about all day long seems to attract those very same feelings and circumstances. I did precisely that for 25 to 30 years. NOW it is time for a change. I see good coming from what has happened to me. But I NOW look at it as one big learning curve and I get to learn it again. The way that works for me! By being me.

Looking forward is part of the new me. I am NOW happier and much more in control of my life. The plans I have are from a place of peace. I now feel care-free, much like when I was a child. I just did it! I feel I can look and visualise the complete article. Looking forward gives me inspiration. Seeing my desires unfold bit by bit. I hope this book provides a stepping stone for others to achieve their desires. Taking a step at a time.

Whilst looking forward I hope to fundraise and write more books for the challenges I have in mind. 'Success in my hands' is a victory over myself. At last I can be myself. Success is part of the journey. It is the process of thinking and acting in a certain way.

I perhaps learnt it the hard way. I am much better than I used to be. The journey NOW is much about setting up a new path to go along. But a path that leads to what I want in my life. No more mazes to wander around, no more wells to fall into. Much more about allowing more to come into my life. Surrendering and putting my hands up and saying 'I allow others to help me move forward to achieve my dreams.'

Independence and choice were two things I always wanted. Through changing my perceptions of myself through the eyes of others, I get to see clearly NOW. My perceptions now create stepping stones. One stone placed in front of the other to get to where I want to. If I look forward and start to view things differently, barriers then are a thing of the past. It is my thinking that creates new way forward.

To me barriers are something that I felt had to overcome, get round, over or under, to break them down. Stepping stones seem much more fun to create. Children would have done this at early ages in streams, I know I did. Place in one in from of the other and watching how the water flowed around them. That to me is much easier than trying to break down a barrier. It was in essence just my mind that held me back. Looking forward is still a mindset but much with a sense of going with the flow of life. When you try to resist it, persist is something that comes to mind. I was always resisting doing things. Now that the brakes are off, I feel free with my thinking and many things can be achieved.

Looking forward also gives me the opportunity to use these new tools for my mind appropriately, with a real sense of purpose. To use them to help myself and others. To give back my knowledge, trusting that others can use them too. The tools are wonderful as they give back the freedom and choice we deserve. I felt at one point I had no real choice or independence: my perception of myself and those around me I suppose was testimony to it or certainly a self fulfilling prophecy.

I just found it difficult to see outside of the box with the luggage I was carrying. I was weighed down with emotional baggage and I could not look forward. The tools now offer hope. They offer a new life for me, along with choice and independence. They give me a means to achieve what I am capable of doing.

Any tool, if used correctly, can give you the edge in anything. The mind is no different: use it well and it will help you achieve pretty much anything. Use it inappropriately and you can self-destruct. I was on that path for quite a few years: I just did not know how to use my brain in the right way.

Looking forward gives me a direction. A new compass setting and more in line with my true self. I suppose looking at my true self is something that I had never done before. I thought if I wanted to do something, I could do it. But the mindset at the time was very different. Misaligned to move forward for what I wanted. Yet I didn't realise I had to really look within and change from inside to enable me to look forward. This change from within has come about at the right time for me.

Change was something that I was trying to do although I was resisting it for fear of the unknown. I was trying to look forward yet bringing the past with me, sabotaging everything I truly wanted in my life. Now I look forward with a sense of creating something new which to me is exciting. A better version of myself. An improved me. The Richard who is just being Rich. The one who explored things as a kid and is doing the same as an adult. Yet without so many inhibitions from what people have said, I decide where I want to go. I can freely choose what I want to do. I can now help others: I could not do that a few years back.

Looking forward and up is now my new direction. It is something that I even think about whilst in the gym: thinking about things that I want. Sometimes just thinking how it would feel with the completion of this book. 'Success in my hands'. A journey that has taken years but now seems so fulfilling and rewarding. I feel I have taken responsibility for myself. No one is to blame. They never were anyway: I just reacted to it all.

Now I allow more things to come into my life. The forward thinking is creative. What more can be done with my new self as it were. Having a coach provides me with a sense of seeing things differently in many areas of my life.

'Progress is seeing the same things differently' (Kevin Laye). Looking forward to things adds a sense of excitement and a little of the unknown. That unknown is there to be explored: the excitement comes from exploring something new. New things are for exploring. Now the fear and anxiety has gone: there is a carefree attitude in exploring. A care free attitude but with a safe approach along with it. Safe because I know where I made my mistakes and I have learned. Stay away from wells and I will be fine: go near them and the answer is obvious.

Looking forward has removed the word disability from my mind and has replaced it with just me. Being me, my true self is who I am. Unique just like everyone else. That true self perhaps wanted to help others. People will help if you ask. I was always asking, always searching and finally I found what I was looking for. My own peace.

Look forward and be in a sense of awe that I can do it. A mind over matter. An overwhelming obsession some might say. Yet that obsession has been the making of me when it could have been the breaking of me. Which do you think?

Looking forward gives me a sense of being able to do things, enabling now, doing the things that I feel I can. Mind and body going forward in one direction. That drive is there again, but this time with a better fuel inside. A fuel that is ignited by passion to do something good with this. The passion I guess was always there: it just needed a way out from within. That way out has been through challenging myself from within and looking inside to get better outer results. Smiling from within and it shows by people smiling back. How cool is that. Something I have never really witnessed and now I seem to see it everywhere I go.

Looking forward adds to a strength that I guess has been there all along. Looking forward gives me the opportunity to create something new for myself. It also gives me a chance to look at my inner strength. Given the fact that there is an inner strength from this process, would it now just be a process of seeing things slightly differently?

Looking forward gives me optimism: I will achieve what I set out to do. This new journey of self, as it were, is fascinating. I have found it inspiring because so many others have done this as well. Many authors have turned things around because they looked within to change their outer not the other way round.

As I have mentioned before, looking forward offers hope. I hope I can make a difference in this world. My physical difference has been a challenge: I had to change my thinking to make a difference in me. Looking forward is an intention: I want to keep moving forward with the ease and flow that I have recently become accustomed to.

That ease and flow seems like a gentle river now: it will keep flowing back to its source. To be kind to others having been kind to myself. It is joyful to see others do so many simple acts of kindness. I never really saw it before. I was too busy looking back at the past and dragging that emotional baggage with me. Smiling gives me a lift and creates a better sense of well-being. So easy and so honest. Fake it and others will know. When it's real and from within others definitely know it.

So looking forward seems to offer so much. Well 'the world is your oyster', some may say. Actually only my thoughts have enabled me to do this. I pretty much have an open mind: I just observe what is going on in people's lives without judging them.

I suppose judging others is a reflection of myself. Also accepting others is a reflection of myself: that's more powerful and inspiring to me. Accepting others just as they are. If I am doing just that—fully accepting myself— the reflection then comes easier. That's something to be grateful for and something to honour and cherish.

So disability has become a unique ability, disabling to enabling and looking forward keeps me moving forward. All going in the direction that my mind and body is going. I am now creating a road to get to somewhere else. Our unique abilities can help us get where we want to go: we all have it in us. It only takes someone else to see it and tell us that is there.

Taking command over my life! Perhaps from seeing things from a different perspective. I now have a greater understanding of what I went through. I do feel that it was meant to be.

The journey of self-development, learning new things about myself and others has been astounding. In one respect, everybody has a unique journey through life. But it is up to us to find the path that works for each of us. The path that I found to peace and enabling myself to do more is awesome. I have never felt so happy as I have over the past few years. I hope it rubs off.

Challenges are there to overcome. Challenges are there for a reason. That reason for me was to show that my physical difference is accepted as part of the whole of me.

Stepping stones to success.

The journey as I move forward is now a new one, exciting and full of adventures. Much like when I was very young and adventures would feel the norm. I feel there are no more barriers. The stepping stones are being placed in front of me day by day as I move towards my intentions. I feel that nothing can stop me now. It is like I am creating my own painting with me in it.

Going with the flow! I now seem to be going with the flow of life. This is new to me but somehow feels really comfortable. The brakes are off this car and it feels great!

Tools for forward thinking.

The tools I have been given have enabled me to do so much. Yet I somehow get to pinch myself in awe of them. I now realise that the tools can only be used if willing to use them. Willing and able. I make myself able by keeping my body in the condition that is optimium for absorbing all this new information.

Setting a new compass direction

Up until I went to Harley street the compass was always spinning round. No definite direction put in place. I had yet to set my own true North, my authentic true North. It was already there: I just hadn't acquired the skills to set it. Much like learning to map read but always forgetting the compass. How would I feel if told time and time again to bring one along to the class but didn't? It would only have been my responsibility to bring it along. Now I realise it is my responsibility to take my life's direction.

Stepping out of the box.

To get out of where I was I had to change my thinking. Get out of the box and stay out of it. Get out of the box and a whole new world opens up. That whole new world comes from a way of thinking. Thinking as a whole being rather than being controlled by outer circumstances. My world at last being created by feeling better. I had to find a better way to think. Out of the box and free.

Smile from within.

This is a term I thought of a while back because of the inside out approach. To me it's simple: smile from within and those on your outside seem to smile back. It truly works. I keep seeing it day in day out as I keep smiling. To me I feel happier inside and I guess that's what people pick up on. I am so looking forward to rest of my life and what it has to offer. Better thinking better living. A new journey with a better future now.

Trust the inner part of you.

Now having realised there is a part of me that feels it knows what is best for me I follow it. A way of knowing. Following my heart. Trusting that all will be ok if I trust.

Follow your bliss.

What makes me happy is now seeing my own change right in front of my eyes. Feeling at peace and at one with myself seems to me the best state to be in. So much of my life has been utter chaos. Now I guess the chaos sowed seeds of some kind to germinate many years later in my adult life. Now though seeds of change have been planted. The old seeds gave me the blues: the new now enables me to look forward. I sense that the season has changed from the coldness of winter, where growth is stunted, to one where abundance arrives everywhere. Everything around me seems to blossom. People seem happier, kindness is visible everywhere.

Being grounded.

Getting back to nature to me signifies being grounded. As I look forward, nature provides me with lots of clues. Nature has a natural flow in it. The seasons flow come and go. Going with the flow as I look forward: this is the way for me now. Why would I want to fight against it after all that has happened?

Acceptance of myself

This is now a reality. By looking forward now I bring acceptance into all that I do and have. People around me feel more comfortable as I move from being someone who did not know how to accept himself to one who is accepting all that is.

Disabling to enabling. Disability to unique ability. Unique ability to just being me.

Being me just as I am. I am Richard. Whole and perfect just as the day I was born. Looking forward: this becomes much of my everyday way of thinking. A way that is perfect just as it is. I was born perfect in each and every way. As I grew up others thought I was imperfect and that's how I then started to think. After 40 years of that conditioning, now I say we look at how we think and how we have an impact on our own lives by thinking a certain way. I feel privileged to be in the presence of those that have helped me to transform my life. I look forward now. ☺

> *We all have our time machines. Some take us back, they're called memories. Some take us forward, they're called dreams."*
>
> **Jeremy Irons**

A final thought to you as you read this book is a simple:

'Thank you' for taking the time to get to know why I just wanted to be ME ☺

Reading List

The following books have helped me with my self-development. Each has given me the means to move forward with my life.

'Tapping the Healer Within' by Roger Callaghan (McGraw Hill 2002)

'The Five minute cure for Public Speaking and other fears' by Roger Callaghan (Balloon View 2008)

'Stop the nightmares of trauma' by Roger Callaghan (Roger Callaghan books)

'Positive Drinking' by Kevin Laye (Hayhouse 2010)

'Tapping for Life' by Janet Thompson (Hayhouse 2010)

'Getting Past OK' by Richard Brodie (Hayhouse 2009)

'Virus of the mind' by Richard Brodie (Hayhouse 2009)

'You can heal your life' by Louise Hay (Hayhouse 2009)

'The biology of belief' by Bruce Lipton (Hayhouse 2009)

'The Power of Intention' by Wayne Dyer (Hayhouse 2008)

'Stop the Excuses' by Wayne Dyer (Hayhouse 2009)

'Excuses Begone' by Wayne Dyer (Hayhouse 2009)

'Change your thoughts, change your life' by Wayne Dyer (Hayhouse 2008)

'Secrets for Success and Inner Peace' by Wayne Dyer (Hayhouse 2006)

'Ask and it is given' by Ester and Jerry Hicks (Hayhouse 2005)

'From Stress to Success' by John F Demartini (Hayhouse 2009)

'You can have what you want' by Michael Neill (Hayhouse 2006)

'Supercoach' by Michael Neill (Hayhouse 2009)

'Instant Confidence' by Paul Mckenna (Bantem Press 2006)

'I can make you Rich' by Paul Mckenna (Bantam Press 2007)

'Change your life in 7 days' by Paul Mckenna (Bantam Press 2004)

'Quit Smoking today' by Paul Mckenna (Bantam Press 2007)

'You will see it when you believe it' by Wayne Dyer (Arrow Books 2005)

'Make your life Great' by Richard Bandler (Harper Collins 2008)

'Get the life you want' by Richard Bandler (Harper Collins 2008)

'Harmonic Wealth' by James Arthur Ray (Sphere 2008)

'The Key' by Joe Vitale (John Wiley & Sons 2008)

'Having it all' by John Assaraf (Simon & Schuster 2003)

'Zero limits' by Joe Vitale (John Wiley & Sons 2007)

'The Secret' by Rhonda Byrne (Simon & Schuster 2006)

'Success through positive mental attitude' by Napoleon Hill and W. Clement Stone (Thorsons 1990

'How to get from where you are to where you want to be' by Jack Canfield (Harper Collins 2007)

'The Science of Success' by Wallace D. Wattles (Sterling 2007)

'Get off your Butt' by Sean Stephenson (Jossey Bass 2009)

'Chicken Soup for the Soul' by Jack Canfield and Mark Victor Hansen (Random House 2000)

'The Compass' by Tammy Kling & John Spencer Ellis (Harper Collins 2007)

'The Key to living the law of attraction' by Jack Canfield and DD Watkins (Orion Books 2008)

'Shared Experiences' by Charlotte Fielder (REACH 2009)

'Out of the Box' by Rob Eastaway (Duncan Baird 2007)

'Speak in Confidence' by Maggie Eyre (Right Way 2008)

'Letting Go' by Lama Surya Das (Bantam 2004)

'The Tao of Warren Buffet' by Marry Buffett & David Clarke (Pocket Books 2007)

'There Is a Spiritual Solution to every problem' by Wayne Dyer (HarperCollins 2001)

'Being Happy' by Andrew Matthews (Media Masters 1988)

'Follow your Heart' by Andre Matthews (Seashell 1997)

'Attractor Factor' by Joe Vitale (John Wiley & Sons 2008)

Websites

www.kevinlaye.co.uk

www.powertochange.me.uk

www.hayhouse.co.uk

www.2calm.com

www.rogercallahan.com

www.atftfoundation.org

www.drwaynedyer.com

www.louisehay.com

www.paulmckenna.com

www.geniuscatalyst.com

www.johnassaraf.com

www.jamesray.com

www.richardbandler.com

www.successinmyhands.teamasea.com

www.brainsync.com

Author Biography

Firstly why did I write 'Success in my hands'? Simply to help me become happier, to start loving a part of me that I didn't and to be free and at peace to be my self.

I have had the overwhelming desire to be happy almost at any cost. I had I guess a sense of an underlying sadness related to my arms. The emotional feelings I wanted to change and be at peace and free from anxiety, depression and the panic attacks that lasted for nearly 30 years.

This book is my opportunity to explain that the very words, feelings and actions have had a direct impact on my behaviour from an early age. Whilst writing the journey has been one of letting go of those negative thoughts and replacing them with happier ones so that I can 'smile' from the inside.

I believed that my happiness was always to come from the 'inside'. I knew why because my sadness was on the inside, all I had to do was reverse it. But I didn't know 'how' I had to learn it and literally change my whole approach to life. Become enabled by changing the thoughts to happier ones. ☺

Printed in the United States
by Baker & Taylor Publisher Services